You're the One Behind the Curtain

You're the One Behind the Curtain

OCD Strategies and My Humorous,
Obsessive Compulsive Life

Jon Davis

To order additional copies of this book, contact:
Xlibris Corporation
1-888-795-4274
www.Xlibris.com
Orders@Xlibris.com
55573

CONTENTS

To Erica, who read this as I was writing it and assured me it didn't sound like the ramblings of a madman (I suspect that she was lying). And to my parents, who made this possible. We miss you guys.

INTRODUCTION

Imagine, if you will, that you're watching a movie with a crazy, evil antagonist. The main character, let's call him James, is being taunted by this evil man all throughout the film. Detective James tracks this madman, trying to get inside his mind and apprehend him. And then, at the climax of the picture, you come to the overused, clichéd surprise ending—the main character and the psycho were one and the same! James was suffering from multiple personality disorder, and he was just messing with himself the entire time.

This is how I want you to view your obsessive compulsive disorder. You feel as though you're in touch with magical forces and you need to repeat actions or perform little rituals to protect yourself or your loved ones. But there are no magical forces. It's all superstitions that you create. Hence the title of this book. There are no outside forces you have to satisfy, no defusing bad thoughts or bad luck by repeating actions, and no OCD gods to appease. There's just you. Obsessive compulsive disorder can be compared to injuring yourself on purpose throughout the day, then trying to heal or tend to your self-inflicted injuries. I want to help you stop injuring yourself in the first place. Any time you feel the need to perform a compulsion, it's just one part of your brain instructing another. In this way, you're like James.

Not that OCD is comparable to multiple personality disorder. In fact, it's an incredibly common ailment. It's estimated that it affects as many as one in forty people. That's quite a large percentage of society. Next time you're at the grocery store, it's probably a safe bet that one of your fellow shoppers has OCD. It's nothing to be ashamed of. Unfortunately, the embarrassment associated with having such bizarre thoughts keeps people from seeking help, and they suffer alone, silently. The average length of time between a person's initial onset of symptoms and seeking professional help is over seven years. When I was first diagnosed, I was surprised that my strange behaviors and thoughts were classified as OCD. Society and the media seem to define OCD as a simple fear of germs. When people think of OCD, an image might come to mind of someone that hates germs and has to keep their belongings arranged in a specific way. Once you learn more about it and suffer with everything it entails, you might hear someone say "I'm so OCD about cleaning my room," and you just kind of want to say "Shut up you idiot. You don't know anything about what it's like to actually deal with the terrible affliction."

I conducted my own little survey to see what the average person thinks of OCD. My questions were phrased "When you think about obsessive compulsive disorder, what comes to mind? If you heard someone had OCD, what would you picture that person doing?" Indeed, of the sixty-five friends, family members, and in some cases complete strangers that responded, over half of them said they thought of some form of washing or cleaning. The most common responses were:

Washing or Cleaning	55%
Repeating Actions	27%
Keeping Things Organized or Arranged a Specific Way	27%
Rechecking Locks or a Stove	23%
Counting	12%
Sticking to a Certain Routine	10%
Flipping Light Switches Multiple Times	7%

When I first began questioning people, it seemed as though every other person mentioned light-switch flipping. Clearly the end results didn't reflect that, but I found it interesting that it was still in the top seven of the twenty-five examples of OCD people gave me. It got me thinking that it probably has something to do with subconscious anxieties that arise when you're suddenly surrounded by darkness. Thoughts of death or a primal fear of being hunted might come to mind, and some people suffering from OCD might want to defuse those fears by repeatedly turning on the lights.

Some of the less frequent responses dealt with alcoholism, gambling, or a sense that a person has done something wrong or offended someone. But I think the results show that most people don't realize that OCD can also deal with bizarre thoughts about subjects such as demonic possession or fear that your morals or intelligence can suddenly, magically change.

That's part of the reason I wanted to write this book. Most OCD help books I've read in the past have dealt more with the fear of germs or the fear of causing an accident. I suffer from OCD, but I hardly have a problem with germs or uncleanness (one look at my kitchen counters or the amount of dust in my bedroom could tell you that). I think my experience with OCD can be summed up by saying that I've superstitiously tried to keep bad things from happening in the future, and it has definitely taken on a very religious theme a lot of the time. It's certainly not always about a fear of God or damnation, but I can relate more to bizarre chants and rituals than I can to excessive washing or rechecking. I've been dealing with it my whole life, and I've repeated actions to ease anxiety of things ranging from school sports, exams, money, severe weather, and nuclear war. It was more of a superstitious, relatively small part of my childhood and young adult life. When I reached the age of twenty-two and suddenly I was finishing up college, about to enter the real world, and my mother passed away, it kicked into high gear. It remained strong for years. At one point when I was twenty-four, I even checked myself into a mental health clinic for a couple weeks because I felt I couldn't function; I was repeating so many everyday actions that I could barely perform daily hygiene or work-related tasks. However, at this point in my life, I feel as though I've analyzed it and can keep it under control without the help of any medication or therapy. There are certain strategies I evoke to combat it, and I'd like to share them with you. Hopefully they can work for you as well.

You shouldn't be embarrassed that you have rituals and superstitions that may have gotten out of hand. Several successful and well-known people suffer from OCD—Howard Hughes, Billy

Bob Thornton, and host of children's game show *Double Dare*, Marc Summers, just to name a few. The world is a scary place, and human beings do not yet have the tools or understanding to comprehend or explain life. No one can tell you why horrible, random things happen to us. But people have been trying to ward off tragedies by performing unrelated rituals since the beginning of mankind. Ancient civilizations would make sacrifices and perform ritualistic dances to keep gods happy and ward off events such as flooding or droughts. Average, everyday people keep lucky charms or wear certain "lucky" articles of clothing before athletic performances to give them a sense of confidence and safety. Some would even argue that religion is a glorified, socially acceptable form of OCD.

With OCD, I've found that there's an aspect of blocking out certain thoughts or distracting yourself from confronting them. Sure, at times you may repeat a trivial action in order to, for example, do well in an upcoming job interview. But at times, you seem to get a bad, unspecific feeling of dread. This is when you have a subconscious thought you don't want to confront. Instead, you distract yourself from this thought and repeat an action in order to defuse your anxiety.

That's part of coming to terms with your role as the person behind the curtain. Figuring out what you're doing back there. At times, when you have a bad feeling about the future, try and identify the thought you don't want to confront instead of immediately performing a senseless action. Not that I'm promoting drug use in any way, but when I was twenty, before I even knew that I had OCD but knew that I thought in a very strange and superstitious way, I had a very enlightening experience with marijuana. I was suddenly unafraid to confront anxiety-provoking thoughts. I was writing what was more or less a journal entry for myself to read once I was no longer under the influence. I wrote the word "death," then noticed that I tapped the end of my pen to my finger three times. So I immediately began to write about how I was just distracting myself from the concept of death to defuse the anxious feelings it brought up.

That's why it's important to keep in mind that your disorder is a result of, at least in part, brain chemistry. That's why pharmaceutical drugs such as Paxil and Prozac can help so much. There are abnormalities in your brain structure and serotonin receptors. It helps to remember that about OCD. Personally, I know that after I eat certain foods, I get more anxious and have the desire to carry out more compulsions. This just proves that it's brain chemistry as opposed to magic. The brain is an extremely powerful organ that we don't fully understand. When you feel like you're a different person because things are "off," or your magic control of the future feels exceptionally real, you have to remember that it's all coming from your head. When you believe in something, it feels real. But magical OCD rules are certainly not.

So at this point in my life, I have it pretty much under control. I can go back to specific experiences with OCD and analyze them. Maybe you just started dealing with the disorder. It got really bad for me about seven and a half years ago. Hopefully I can teach you what I've learned from my experience with it; hopefully my strategies can work for you. I do want to warn, however, that if you feel very susceptible to new forms of compulsions, you may not want to get ideas from me. My OCD has been constantly evolving and changing since I was a little kid, and I'm always finding new ways to torture myself.

As you read my life story, I'll probably come across as a very Christian person. Or at least it will seem that way at earlier points in my life. So I want to state now what my beliefs are. I believe that there's possibly some higher form of intelligence or a creator, but not the God of Christianity with all the jealousy and wrath. In America, we become so brainwashed with the idea of the Christian God, Jesus, Satan, heaven, and hell that we almost forget about the rest of the world. Christianity isn't even the world's biggest religion any more. So are the billions of Muslims, Hindus, Buddhists, Jews, etc., going to hell when they die simply because they were brought up to follow the incorrect religion? According to the Christian Bible, they would be. That seems to me an unfair way to look at the world. And of course, there are the millions of horrible things that happen on a daily basis. Seems hard to believe in a loving God when you take into consideration everything that happens on our planet. And don't give me the free will argument, free will has nothing to do with terminally ill children and tsunamis. And if the Lord works in mysterious ways, at the very least we should know the reason behind all the suffering in the world, instead of accepting it at face value.

Some say that you have to believe, despite scientific findings and horrible acts of violence, and then you are rewarded for your faith. That again seems unfair to me; with so much evidence against stories found in the Bible, it seems light years beyond unfair to be punished for not believing if God is hiding. As I was stating earlier, I think religion gives people a sense of comfort and protection from negative events. Religion also has mind chants and rituals; it just isn't as out of hand and bizarre as it is with OCD.

But I also think religion serves as a means to keep people in line and to give them a sense of guilt over misdeeds. At times, this can be too extreme. Growing up, I didn't see God as someone to protect me, I saw him as someone to punish me for being bad or for having bad thoughts. The idea of a God monitoring your thoughts, ready to punish you eternally if you're a bad person, can really screw with the mind of someone with the scrupulous form of OCD. Just earlier today, I was talking to someone who told me that her eight-year-old daughter has been worrying (to the point of crying) about saying bad things in her mind and thinking that God might hear them and be angry or punish her. Way to go, religion!

All of that being said, the one thing that has been the backbone of my OCD since the beginning is a fear of hell. The concept of Hades seems pretty unrealistic to me at this point in my life, but I still have lingering shades of belief in the possibility that it exists, and this keeps me wanting to repeat thoughts or actions. It all started when I was a kid, and I saw for the first time television programs about individuals who had spent a brief amount of time clinically dead, only to be revived with stories about visiting a heaven or hell. Some of the people who believed they had gone to hell were so convinced it was a real experience that they turned their lives around and became devout Christians.

A few years ago, I purchased a book about several different people who believed they visited hell. What I found interesting was that everyone's experience with hell was completely different. Some people reported flames; others found themselves in dark nothingness. One man even said he was forced to work on an assembly line and wasn't able to keep up the pace. Now, if all these people were genuinely going to hell, why would it be a totally different experience for them individually? Nowhere in the Bible does it say everyone will go to their own personal hell. It talks about it being a place of fire, cut-and-dried. The only reason everyone's experience would be different is if they were actually just having their own individual dreams while they were on the verge of brain death—individual dreams based on who they were and their life experiences.

All arguments aside about memory being the function of a brain you wouldn't have with you in the afterlife, I was recently discussing the concept of near-death experiences with a friend who knows a good deal about the brain. He informed me that when people are on the verge of death, the brain releases all of its natural hallucinogens and opiates in order to make the experience of death less frightening and painful. So this could easily explain visits to an alleged heaven or hell. If someone has a guilty conscience, their death dream may be some strange vision of punishment. I think the reason hell is described in the Bible as a place of fire and brimstone, or a "lake of fire," is because it was written by people thousands of years ago, when fire was an unexplainable, painful phenomenon.

As you get to my examples of OCD once I get into my twenties, I'm going to sound exceptionally strange. Someone who fears that his thoughts and actions might be influenced by Satan. The only thing I can state to justify that is my thoughts were not all that different from someone who prays to God and believes it can have positive effects. People pray to God for good things to happen in the future, for health of loved ones, and for help in physical or mental skills. If that's possible, and there is a Satan, why couldn't he have the same influence? That's the way I felt when it got really out of hand.

So I have ten strategies to think about whenever you have the urge to act out a compulsion. Some of them are actions you can do; others are more of questions to ask yourself and consider whenever you seem to think you control the uncontrollable. Try to consult them whenever your OCD is bothering you, and try and keep them in mind as you struggle with OCD on a daily basis. They will come up again as I go through the history of my life and my struggle with the disorder. I hope that these strategies can apply to you and your experience with OCD. They may seem a little specific to my exact form of the disorder, but I think they can apply to all forms of OCD in general. And I do actually use these. The other night, I got a bad feeling when I clicked my mouse on a picture online and really felt I had to do it again. I read through this list of ten after I had been stressed about it for a while and found that I did indeed go through eight out of ten in my mind.

CHAPTER 1

Strategies

1. Time is on your side.

This may be obvious, but if you get yourself to ignore your desire to perform a compulsion, it eventually goes away. A few different times in my life, I've decided to officially stop repeating compulsive actions so that I could try to eliminate the stress involved with repeating something over and over. It lasted for a year, both times. It may be a little discouraging that stress got to me after a while and I eventually folded, but it is one of the most effective strategies I've ever tried.

The reason this works so well is that with time, it just becomes more and more powerful. At first, it's "Come on, you've gone a few weeks without repeating anything, don't give that up now." Then eventually, it's months, or even a year. You build up many experiences ignoring really powerful urges to perform compulsions. If you make it months without repeating anything, you don't want to give that all up and start from scratch all over again. You don't want all that work to be for nothing. And when you get really bad feelings, you think "I've ignored plenty of really bad feelings over the past six months and everything has been okay, I'm not going to give in to this one. After a few days, I'll go back to feeling like myself."

Even smaller goals work. If you tell yourself that you're not going to repeat anything for an hour, your stress over repeating something fades, and by the time an hour passes, you may not even feel like repeating it any more. Or even a day. Wake up in the morning and tell yourself, "No acting out compulsions all day today." The next day, after a full night's sleep, you probably won't be able to remember all of the things you wanted to repeat. And of course, if you forget one of the things you had to repeat, it suddenly doesn't count. Because you knew it was meaningless in the first place.

A strategy I've found to be effective recently is to put off repeating compulsions for one week. Start, for example, on a Monday morning and tell yourself that no matter how badly you want to perform a compulsion, you have to save it for the following Monday morning. It eases your stress a little to think that you will indeed be able to repeat yourself if you just wait a few days. Personally, I've found that realizing you can indeed repeat your action if you just wait a few days almost yields the same sense of relief as actually repeating the action. A week seems like a nice block of time because when you consider giving in to your OCD, you ask yourself "You're trying to quit this shit for good, and you can't make it a couple of days?" And most importantly, by the time a week rolls around, you pretty much have no desire to repeat your compulsions or you've forgotten about some of them entirely.

When you ignore the desire to repeat something, it's very stressful at first. But with time, you go back to feeling like yourself. Not to mention the fact that new compulsions eventually take the place of big ones you felt like you couldn't get over. When you try not to repeat something, you think of all kinds of logical reasons why there's no reason to repeat some trivial action. You tell yourself it's just OCD, you analyze why exactly it upset you in the first place, and you think about other people and the fact that they don't need to repeat actions to keep bad luck away. And when a new compulsion comes along, all the things you told yourself about the original compulsion become true, and it doesn't even bother you any more.

No matter how scary or real your anxiety is, it always fades away with time. Even if you're convinced that you're suddenly a new person, you always go back to feeling like yourself. You've been yourself for years, after all.

2. Write down what's causing you stress, tell someone about it, or read about OCD.

Anything you can do to remind yourself that you have a mental illness works wonders. Sometimes, I spend hours fighting the urge to repeat some trivial action because I think it will have an effect on the unrelated future. When I write down what it is that's bothering me, and what I want to repeat, it reminds me of how illogical it sounds. It reminds me that I have OCD. And I start to feel better.

Explaining your compulsion to someone you know also works. Because when you explain it, you don't explain it as though you believe you have some magical effect on the future. It's more along the lines of "I have this thing called obsessive compulsive disorder, and right now I'm fighting the urge to . . . . Isn't that funny?" Talking about your problems always helps.

Reading about OCD also helps because it serves to remind you that you have a disorder, and you're certainly not alone in the suffering it causes. It helps to read a quick summary of what OCD is, what causes it, and other people's experiences. This is a strategy I've used multiple times in my life when my compulsions got out of hand. I read about OCD for a while, and I was suddenly much more able to keep things under control.

3. Analyze the real concerns behind your uneasy feeling.

For a while, I kept a list of many of the actions I had the urge to repeat. Eventually I looked at the entries on the list and thought about the subconscious concerns they must have evoked. For example, whenever I saw the birth and death years of someone in a newspaper article or on television, I found myself repeatedly doing the quick math in my mind to figure out how long they lived. Probably because of the anxiety and uncertainty regarding the concept of death. I wanted to defuse my fear of death and distract myself from confronting my own mortality by occupying myself with math. I found myself doing the same thing regarding math involving my finances and bank accounts. Same basic principle—I have anxiety about my future and monetary situation. So I would start to get a bad feeling about death or the future, and I would have to repeat the math until things felt "just right." Another example is a time I was reading about New York and found myself repeating an action. Probably because I started thinking about 9/11 and was worried about any possible future terrorist attacks.

So when you find yourself repeating an action, ask yourself why you want to. Confront your fears instead. Why are you so convinced you're going to cause some terrible accident? Is it because you feel a lot of guilt about something? The objects that you have to keep aligned in order to protect your loved ones—what kinds of memories do they bring up?

4. Can you make your compulsion impossible to act out?

I recommend that you immediately ask yourself this question when you're bothered by a compulsion. Because if the answer is yes, it works wonders. When I was a junior in college, I was about to write a paper for an English class. I kept getting a bad feeling every time I started to write my opening sentence. I couldn't concentrate because everything felt "off" as I kept writing and scratching out the first word on this "magic" sheet of paper. I switched to a brand new sheet of paper but had to keep making little pen marks on the original because my stressful feeling wouldn't go away. Eventually I just ripped it up and flushed it down the toilet so that changing the amount of times I wrote on it was no longer an option.

This is something I was thinking about recently when I had the desire to readjust a pocket flap on a pair of shorts I was wearing. I eventually decided that rather than succumbing to my compulsion and breaking my streak of not repeating actions, I would throw my shorts in a dumpster somewhere and never see them again. I didn't actually end up doing this, but as soon as I decided I would get rid of them before readjusting the pocket, it was a lot easier to ignore the desire. (They were a cheap pair of shorts, probably ten years old. Throwing them away because of OCD wouldn't have been as extreme as it may sound.)

If you are able to make your compulsion impossible to act out, it helps you for a couple of reasons. Obviously, the stress involved with wanting to repeat the action will no longer exist. But also, it will show you that your bad feeling will magically go away, and nothing bad will happen as a result. It helps to prove that there's no magic or truth behind your strange little desires.

5. Consider your actual compulsions. You're just torturing yourself, and you never have to do anything too extreme.

Personally, I find that the things I want to repeat are actions I don't want to do because they would be embarrassing, draw attention to myself, or have negative consequences on my life. This will come up a lot as I go through my OCD life history. Instead of simple things that no one would notice, my compulsions often involve sounding or looking foolish by repeating words or actions around people who are unaware that I have OCD, or denying myself something I want because of OCD. Since I'm the one behind the curtain, I'm just making life harder for myself. That's just the kind of personality I have. I torture myself; I sabotage myself. I'm guessing you might be the same way if you have OCD. An example that comes to mind is difficulty sleeping. On nights that it doesn't matter how much sleep I get, I sleep like a baby. Two times last summer, I woke up at maybe 6:00 a.m. to spend twelve hours or more driving across the country. On each of these nights, I literally got maybe an hour or two of sleep. Why? Because it mattered. I wanted to be alert, driving on the highway all day. I wanted to be able to drive several hours and not have to sleep shortly into my trip. (And of course, when it was maybe 5:30 a.m. and my alarm was going to sound in half an hour, I fell asleep. Because at that point, it didn't matter if I fell asleep.) I sabotaged myself. I laid in bed all night torturing myself, not being able to sleep simply because I wanted to, simply because I was worried about it, simply because I needed to sleep that night.

And of course, your compulsions are never anything too inappropriate or illegal. I'm guessing you've never had to repeat an action that might lead to a serious accident. You never get the compulsion to go up to a stranger in a restaurant and throw hot soup in his face. You never have to throw away something you purchased for a thousand dollars because you have a bad feeling about it. You never get the sensation that unless you throw a brick at a nearby police officer, nuclear war will happen tomorrow. Not because you're lucky that the OCD demons give you simple tasks to perform, but because YOU'RE deciding exactly what you have to do to make yourself feel better.

Here are a few personal examples to illustrate my point. The other night, after I shut my garage door, I got a bad feeling and wanted to close it again. But I ignored it and walked up to my condo. Of course, this ended up being a very strong feeling that was hard to ignore. This is because it would have been a very involved action to repeat. It's not something I could repeat alone in my condo, with no one watching. I would have to walk back to my garage, all the while risking getting another bad feeling and having to repeat the walk. Not to mention the fact that my neighbors might see me and wonder why I was repeatedly walking to my garage.

I've also noticed that right before I'm in social situations, I get a strong feeling and want to repeat something. This is just my way of sabotaging myself when I'm about to interact with people. I'll obviously be nervous and distracted if I'm concentrating on wanting to repeat an action during a time that I'm supposed to be having fun with friends. So I get the urge to repeat something in order to make my social experience less pleasurable.

6. Other people don't realize they're changing the future?

This is a question you can ask yourself when you feel like repeating an action. If you believe that your trivial little actions control huge events in the future, is that the way it is for everyone? Little does the rest of the world know, sometimes when they cross the threshold of a room, they suddenly turn into an evil person. Or because they didn't lock their door three times, they caused a serious car accident for a relative. Good thing you're special and in touch with the magical forces that rule the world—you get to protect yourself from things like that.

Of course that isn't true. So take comfort in the fact that most people have their anxiety under control, they don't engage in rituals, and they get by just fine. If you hear that someone was in an accident, do you think "they must not have tapped their door knob the right amount of times this morning"? No, of course you don't.

7. Look at your life in a larger perspective; everything's not going to change all of the sudden.

Sometimes with OCD, we get caught up on some trivial action of everyday life. We think not repeating something is going to change us or change the future forever. Sometimes it's important to look at the bigger picture. Say you're twenty-five years old. You have an OCD moment, and you're convinced you're going to be a different person all of the sudden unless you repeat an action. Think beyond that day. Say to yourself, "I've been a certain person for twenty-five years. Now, because of the amount of times I watched the minutes on a digital clock change, I'm going to be someone else for the next sixty years? I totally just changed the future? Funny, I've never turned into a completely different person at any other point in my life."

8. You don't control such huge events.

People with OCD believe they control enormous, life-altering, worldwide events. This is another strategy where you need to look at the big picture. Obsessive compulsives have rituals that they believe prevent the deaths of their loved ones, terrorist attacks, etc.

Personally, some of my rituals or mind chants have been to prevent nuclear war, terrorist attacks, even World War III. Even recently, when I'm at a point in my life where I have an IRA, I find myself superstitiously trying to make the stock market perform well.

When I think about it logically, it makes me feel pretty foolish. "Little do these people reporting at CNN know, it's actually the thoughts I'm repeating that's affecting stocks today . . ." Some of the things you worry about and try to prevent affect billions of people in the world. You're not a god. You have nothing to do with the prevention of most things.

9. If you're religious, make a deal with God that if you repeat a certain action, it will mean that you want to be damned.

That might sound a little strange, but a few years ago, it was one of my most effective strategies. Because my OCD is rooted so much in the fear of hell, the ultimate way to get myself to stop repeating actions is if I believed it would damn me. This is something I started doing in late 2002, and I felt as though I had discovered a loophole in my OCD.

Let's say, for example, that I put a plate away in a cabinet and got a bad feeling about the future. I would say in my mind "God or anyone listening, if I move that plate to erase my anxious feeling, Satan can have my soul." So that would scare me out of moving it. If you believe in a God more powerful than your OCD (which, deep down, you know is just a mental disorder), you can use that to your advantage in making little "deals" that could stop you from repeating actions.

10. See it all as a mental disorder. KNOWING it's fake is the ultimate strategy.

This is where I'd like to think I am, with my experience with OCD, for the most part. You have several tools now to analyze what's bothering you when OCD is strong. You have to keep in mind that it's all in your head. It's not coming from anywhere else, just regions of your brain that you may be afraid to confront. See it as a disease, not as superstitious magic. Not as some power you've tapped into that everyone else seems to be oblivious to.

I'm sure you're familiar with the sense of relief that comes with repeating an action. A sense that things are back to normal, and everything is going to be okay. Instead of feeling this way because you perform a compulsion, you need to feel this way because you know it's all fake. And that's the ultimate strategy. The idea that it's all a mental disorder and none of the magic is real can become like a bulletproof vest for you, and your obsessions and anxious thoughts will bounce off of you like bullets.

So now let me take you through the history of my experience with OCD. What I've done, to hopefully make it more entertaining, is told it as more of a life story. I tried to think of the most humorous or entertaining stories from my life and included them as I talk about the different examples and evolution of my OCD. Hopefully you can laugh a little in this time of dealing with your stressful disorder. A lot of these stories have absolutely nothing to do with the disorder, but I thought it would make a better book than simply a list of my many different obsessions and compulsions. Early on, it may seem there are just as many random stories as there are stories about OCD. But that will change later in the book. As I said, it was a smaller part of my childhood, but really got out of control in my twenties. By the end, you'll see why I felt I had the right to compose a whole book on the subject.

CHAPTER 2

The Grade School Years and
My Fear of the Unexplained

April 6, 1978. Bob and Annette Davis find themselves at the home of Margaret Friers, Annette's aunt, celebrating her forty-sixth birthday. At some point in the evening, Bob and Annette sneak off to a closet to engage in a little sexual intercourse. Nine months later, I arrive. Why do I know the details of my conception? I don't know, I guess I had a pretty open family.

I was born in Wheaton, Illinois, a western suburb of Chicago. My parents had already made a couple of children when I showed up: nine-year-old Lori and five-year-old Amy. The production of children ceased with me, because it was clear early on that I would have been impossible to top. My father worked for an advertising agency downtown Chicago. This job was fun for me throughout my childhood—several trips to California, visiting the sets of Nintendo and McDonalds commercials. Plus, when I was maybe eight, I was really into the Short Circuit movies, with the sassy robot Johnny Five. My dad had worked on a commercial with Tim Blaney, the man who provided Johnny Five's voice. So on my birthday, he had Tim call me and pretend to be Johnny Five. The best part was when I told him I got a Casio keyboard as a birthday gift, and he responded "My cousin was a Casio!"

My mom stayed home to raise us. It's interesting these days how many laws there are regarding children and car seats, and the grief pop stars get when they drive with a child on their lap for a moment. When I was a small child running errands with my mom, I just sat next to her on the fold-down armrest, not belted in at all.

According to her, I actually just stood on the armrest dancing and singing along to songs on the radio while she was driving. Scientists agree that OCD is at least somewhat inherited. Brain structure and neurochemistry that causes OCD can be passed along genetically. My mother definitely had some obsessive compulsive tendencies. All of the digital clocks in our house had to be synchronized, almost to the second. Lori was driven crazy by the fact that the two light switches in her bedroom had to be in the correct positions—down when the light was off, up when it was on. My sisters' shared bedroom was the entire upper level of our house, so there was a light switch at the base of the stairs leading up to the room, and another in the room itself. Lori was actually forced to return to her room at times to keep the switches synchronized. My mom also seemed to be pretty superstitious at times, but in a more lighthearted way. She was a pretty big sports fan, and of course in the early '90s, the Chicago Bulls were a fantastic dynasty. During important playoff games, she would suddenly disappear for several minutes at a time. Eventually, when we started inquiring each other as to where she had gone, we heard "they started winning when I came down here, so I can't leave this room!" from the basement.

The main thing I remember from my very early years is that I was kind of the neighborhood mischievous kid. There were several children a few years younger than myself, and I seemed to take advantage of that by telling them to do things they wouldn't realize would land them in trouble. There was a young boy that lived directly across the street from us. One day while we were playing, I informed him that a killer farmer lived in my basement. Perhaps it was just the ghost of a killer farmer; I don't remember the details. Either way, the story was that there was a killer farmer lurking in our home, maybe chasing me around every once in a while. The morning after I disclosed this whopper, my parents got a call from the boy's father. Turns out he couldn't sleep all night because he was afraid of the killer farmer across the street. He came over with his dad, and I had to show him that there was indeed no such farmer.

It was this type of story that earned me a reputation of being the young kid that parents were weary about. I remember knocking on my friend's door to see if he could play. He asked his mother "Can I play with that Davis kid?" in such a way that it was clear to me he was repeating his parents from a time they had discussed my antics in a negative way. There are a few serious things I did or lied about that I'd rather not even mention. I recalled several memories of me messing with people as I thought about my life story. As you'll see through my childhood and into my teenage years, it was kind of a theme with me. Which is interesting, considering obsessive compulsive disorder is just me messing with myself. Perhaps the psychic at Lori's bachelorette party was right when she told Lori that her brother likes power and likes messing with people (although she also told her I would end up being a cop).

When I started school, I was exceptionally shy. That may sound surprising given my little resume of neighborhood troublemaking. It wasn't until first grade that I met a fellow weirdo named Stefan and started acting goofy in school. I began to get in trouble for talking to people I was seated near or getting sent into the hallway for yelling things like "Purple potato!" in the middle of quiet time.

One thing about my obsessive compulsive personality, especially as a child, was my fascination with the paranormal. I was obsessed with stories of ghosts and other strange phenomena during my childhood. It seems like every time I started hanging out with a new friend, it wasn't long before I was talking about things such as ghosts and psychic powers. At the same time, these subjects frightened me. There were certain images on television programs about the unexplained that I would actually look away from, such as crop circles. I felt as though if they weren't understood, it was possible that looking at them would have some kind of negative effect on me. My OCD had a similar theme. I was worried about things I didn't understand, such as God or misfortune.

One of my earliest memories of my "magical" thinking is documented in a photo album of mine. I was on a train ride with my sisters and grandmother from Illinois to California at age seven. I had a new camera along with me, a gift from my grandma. It was a cheap little thing with a slot for flashbulb sticks. Little rows of eight bulbs that would burst one at a time when you wanted to take pictures in dark conditions. Remember those? I think I may have been the only person to ever own one.

At one of the stops, my grandma, sisters, and myself got out to walk around. A machine was slowly scrolling alongside the cars of our train, cleaning it. I thought it was a nifty-looking machine, so I decided to take one picture of it. But after I snapped that first shot, it wasn't enough. I got a "bad" feeling about the future and had to take another. I thought taking another picture would cancel out the bad feeling I had, and good things would be in store for me in the long run. But a second picture didn't make my weary feeling go away, so I ended up taking three.

And do you know what was really going on here, partially? I was forcing myself to do something that I didn't want to do. I had maybe a couple rolls of film, and I wanted to save them for pictures of our final destination, not the train ride. And I didn't want my family looking at the pictures later, thinking, "Why would he take so many pictures of a train-cleaning machine?" In an indirect, analytical way, that's why I took so many pictures. Because I only wanted to take one, for multiple reasons.

Of course, from a magical-thinking, OCD standpoint, I took several pictures to make my future good. But it just so happened that to make my future good, I had to force myself to do something that I didn't want to do. I could have been repeating the amount of steps I took when we were at this train stop, but that would have been too easy. There's another example of this later in the same photo album. I have seven pictures taken looking out of an airplane window, when I probably wanted to take one or two.

In second grade, an IQ test was given to all the students in both second-grade classes at my elementary school. The four or five students that scored the highest were put into a special program that met once a week, TAG (talented and gifted). They would meet for an hour every Wednesday and discuss things such as advertising, optical illusions, and tessellation. I ended up being one of the kids in this program throughout grade school. The only reason I'm bringing this up is to give you some kind of insurance. You may not be getting advice from some insane idiot but, rather, from someone who scored highly on an IQ test at some point in the '80s.

There are a few other examples I can recall from this time that were simple little rituals I felt I had to do in order to keep bad things from happening to me. Nothing major, just little superstitions. I always had a good feeling about the number 3; I'm not exactly sure why. Three or multiples of three. After brushing my teeth, I had to tap my toothbrush to the sink nine times. Whenever I put my bike in our garage and shut the electric garage door, I had to make sure to touch a certain spot on our deck before the door completely shut behind me. There wasn't a lot of thought put into these; I just felt better about things in general if I did them. It was my way of defusing a general feeling of anxiety about life.

I remember feeling as though the words I spoke carried some kind of importance. As though saying something might actually make it true, or the forces at work (God, I suppose) would hear me say something and make it officially true. For example, if I were ever to say "Oh, I'm so stupid!" out of frustration, I would have to make sure and say "I'm not stupid" to cancel it out. Otherwise, I felt I suddenly might actually become stupid. I think, at times, I would also try to cancel out words I spoke by saying them backwards.

It wasn't just speaking things aloud that bothered me; thinking them caused me some discomfort as well. Pink Floyd's "Another Brick in the Wall" was popular at this time, and it included the line "we don't need no education." If I thought that line—spoke it in my mind, if you will—I had to follow it up by thinking "I DO need an education. An education is important and something I need in life" (or something along those lines; it's been twenty years). I didn't want the forces at work to decide "Well fine, if you don't need no education, we'll deprive you of one!" and take away my education or my ability to learn. Another song, Real Life's "Send Me an Angel" from such movies as *Rad* and *Teen Wolf Too*, caused me some stress as well. If I found myself saying "Send me an angel" out loud, I would follow it up by saying "Don't have to send me an angel" just to make sure some angel wasn't going to possess me or change my life. This reflected my fear and lack of understanding of religion in general. It was similar to a time in gym class when my friend Kevin made the sign of the cross on my chest before I was timed doing sit-ups. Even that caused me discomfort and made me fear that my life would be affected or I would be a different person because of some sort of official Christian blessing.

Touching the bottom of my feet is something I can recall doing at this time as well. If I had a bad feeling, it was as though there were evil spirits attached to me that I had to defuse. Touching the bottom of my feet would get the negative energy off my body, and I'd be "refreshed," so to speak. Of course it was never anything too extreme. I never suddenly had to defuse myself by leaving my house or school and touching the ground. Just something simple I could do that no one would really notice. I'll get into more examples of defusing negative energy from myself later.

At one point in third grade, right after lunch, all the kids and our teacher returned to the classroom, and I burped as loud as I possibly could. All the children laughed, and my teacher, Mrs. Ream, angrily asked, "Who did that?!"

Several students replied, "Jon!"

"Well, maybe you should go to the office and think about that for a while!" Mrs. Ream decided.

By the time I got to the office, I was crying because I was in trouble. So when I walked up to the main desk, the secretary concernedly asked what was wrong, worrying that I may be hurt.

"I burped really loud," I informed her in a pathetic, high-pitched voice.

She rolled her eyes and said something along the lines of "Just sit on the bench for a while then, you burping jackass."

I don't know why kids are so quick to tattletale. Just like a time in fourth grade when we were eating our lunch in the classroom for some reason. I guess the cafeteria was being used for something else that day. There were no adults in the room, so I started throwing pieces of salami from my sandwich up against the blackboard. They would stick, leaving small greasy circles when I peeled them off.

Of course, when Mrs. Mueller returned and asked how lunch went, a little redheaded girl named Noel immediately responded, "Jon was throwing salami at the chalkboard!"

Some people are just tools that way. There was a boy that lived about a block away from me. He had been homeschooled for a few years and was in my Cub Scout troop. He was an odd and hyper child, and I didn't particularly enjoy his company. One afternoon, he called to ask if I could play, and I looked around the room for an excuse to get out of it.

"Well . . . . my cat's sick" was the best I could do.

"Can you come over to my house then?"

"I should probably stay here and take care of my cat." I don't think he called back after that.

It was around this time that televised tales of the unexplained affected my anxiety yet again. This time, it was cases of alien abduction. I saw reenactments of people being paralyzed while creepy little aliens performed odd experiments on them, often times associated with their reproductive systems. As a consequence, I spent a good deal of time being afraid that I might get abducted. I remember fearing that I would wake up in the middle of the night, only to find that one of those short aliens with the big black eyes was on top of me, having sex with me. And my virginity would be taken, instead of during some hypothetical romantic encounter with a girl ten years in the future, by some asshole alien.

It was as I reached the age of ten or so that I started worrying more about death, Satan, and the afterlife. This was reflected in my OCD thoughts and rituals. My family didn't go to church, and I was worried I might somehow be punished for that. This was when I became concerned about stories of the clinically dead revived with tales of visiting heaven or hell. (I really should have avoided *Unsolved Mysteries* altogether.) I found myself suddenly afraid of death, demons, and damnation.

So I felt as though I had to make sure that the forces monitoring my thoughts would not be under the impression that I wanted Satan to have my soul when I died. I remember having to say in my mind, "The devil may not have my soul unless I jump off the Sears

Tower." A strange and specific set of circumstances indeed, but I found that to be the case a lot with my mind chants. I suppose I wanted to make it exceptionally clear that I didn't want to go to hell when I died, so I picked something that was obviously never going to happen. Hilariously enough, I started worrying that maybe someday I'd be visiting the Sears Tower with my family, and on the way out, I'd jump over the last couple stairs onto the sidewalk. And this would officially count as jumping off the Sears Tower, and I'd be damned. But I'm pretty sure I never accidentally jumped off any part of the Sears Tower, so I'll see you in heaven.

In fourth grade, I began to spend a lot of time with a pair of brothers who would become my best friends for five years. John Gordon was in my grade and lived just down the street. Matt, his younger brother, was two years behind us. From 1989 until 1994, when they moved to California, we more or less spent all our time hanging out with each other unless we were in school or sleeping. In 1990, a boy named E. J. moved in a few houses away from us, and our trio became a foursome. It was a wonderful five years of video games, fire, skateboarding, sports, remote-control cars, Ninja Turtles, water balloons, pornography, crappy early-'90s movies, board games, and mischief.

Mischief, like the time Matt and I decided to hide behind a set of bushes with two small super-bounce balls. The plan was to throw the balls in front of cars leaving work from the out-of-place plastics factory behind my house to see how far we could get them to bounce down Union Avenue (in broad daylight). It didn't take more than a handful of cars before someone stopped to confront us.

After our balls bounced off the front of a large van, it came to a screeching halt, and an angry middle-aged woman emerged. Looking back now, our reaction to this situation is very amusing to me. Obviously, as soon as the van stopped, Matt and I should have sprinted away. As if some middle-aged woman is going to sprint several blocks after two kids, leaving her running vehicle stopped in the middle of the street. But we just stood there, ready to take it.

She started yelling at us, asking where we lived. I was afraid of being grounded and wouldn't provide her with any information, so I started walking quickly in the direction of my house. I looked behind me after I had passed a few houses and saw she was following me, maybe thirty feet on my tail. I would find out later that after I started walking away, she asked Matt what my home phone number was, and *he actually gave her my real number.* Brilliant kids, I tell you! How hard would it have been for him to give her a fake'un?

There was a house almost directly across the street from mine in which the Murray family lived. Our families were pretty close. E. J.'s house was directly behind the Murray's, on the next street over. So whenever I came to and from E. J.'s, I would just cut through the Murray's driveway and walk through their backyard. When I got in front of the Murray's, the angry lady was still on my tail. So I sprinted up their driveway, through the backyard, through E. J.'s yard, and kept going to the nearby wilderness trail. From her point of view, however, I was sprinting to my own home. When I sprinted up the driveway, she was too far behind me to see that I continued through the backyard. So when she got to the back porch of the Murray household, she was greeted by their dog, Shamrock. Shamrock, unaware of who this unfamiliar, angry woman was, proceeded to bite the poor lady. Luckily, I wasn't sued. Just grounded for a little while.

Just as I had done with all my previous friends, I started bringing up the paranormal with the Gordons, and for some reason, we ended up discussing psychic abilities a lot. If John and I both just happened to say something at the same time, we would immediately say "Psychic!" Of course, we said this at the same time as well, so then we would say, in unison, "Psychic again!" Followed up by several more repeats of "Psychic *again!*" Each more enthusiastic than the last, as we kept saying "Psychic again!" at the same time. Idiots.

Along similar lines, Matt and I oftentimes didn't believe the things we told one another. To be more convincing, since we were still very young and feared a punishing God, we would sometimes say "I swear to God." But we found loopholes in order to trick each other. We would cross our fingers behind our backs as we "swore to God," or we would say, "No, I didn't say I swear to God, I said I 'swearta got,' which is just nonsense, so it doesn't count!" So eventually, if someone was doubted, that person would immediately whip his hands out in front of his face, showing the fingers weren't crossed, and say "*I-swear-to-God!*" Emphasizing every little syllable to prove he was actually swearing to God.

Little did Matt know, I was also saying strange chants to God in my mind on a daily basis. OCD suddenly became a lot stronger in fifth grade, and I think it's likely this was because my life was getting a tad more stressful. Not that fifth graders have much to be stressed about, but I was about to move from grade school to middle school. Sixth grade would be a bunch of kids from other schools I had never met, harder classes, six-foot-tall eighth graders, and girls with boobs. So as I began to worry more about life in general, I started with my first significant mind chant. I suddenly felt as though I had to apologize to God if I were to sin. I don't remember exactly what I defined as "sinning" back then. Maybe swearing, maybe thinking something blasphemous like "Screw you, God!" Not because I was actually angry at God, but just as a way of messing with myself, since I was afraid of hell. I remember that if I looked at something I perceived to be evil, I had to apologize to God. Even strange-looking graffiti on a building warranted an apology. Because somehow, I related graffiti to Satan. At this point in my ten-year life, I was pretty uneducated on what a gang was. I just knew they were made up of "bad" kids and, therefore, represented evil. I also thought gangs were into Satanism, and that strange graffiti symbols of crowns and whatnot were Satanic symbols. In fifth grade, there were a few places in my hometown that were suddenly covered in strange graffiti. And honestly, looking back, they may have consisted of anti-God symbols, such as upside-down crosses and sets of 6s. Maybe there were some spray-pantin' punks in extremely religious Wheaton that thought they were Satanists.

As a matter of fact, here's a little story regarding how uneducated and afraid us youngsters were when it came to gangs in the early '90s. In probably sixth grade, John, E. J., and myself were hanging out by the Illinois Prairie Path, which ran behind John's backyard.

This is an extremely long bike/running path in DuPage County; it used to be a railroad track. We were standing around, and a couple older teens with long hair and death metal T-shirts rode by us on one of those mini motorbikes. They were staring at us as they drove by, quite possibly embarrassed that they were on a motorcycle meant for children. For some reason, I flashed that surfer "hang lose" sign (pinky and thumb sticking out), and they slammed on their brakes, skidding along the small white gravel of the Prairie Path. E. J., John, and I took off sprinting back to John's house. When we got inside, we were wondering why they would have stopped, and I told them about my hand gesture. E. J. was very upset—"Damn it! It's called Latin Kings, if you flash them the wrong hand signal, they hunt you down and kill you!" Then we were seriously worried that we might be murdered. Of course, we never saw them again.

Here is what I can recall about my actual mind chants. It started with "Sorry God, I love Jesus, I have seen an aquarium before today." I know that last part sounds extremely strange. This stemmed from by belief that after talking to God, my next thought had to be neutral or positive. I guess I felt as though after praying, my thoughts were still monitored for a few seconds. So I came up with something neutral, probably at a time when I was sitting near an aquarium. This was ineffective anyway because my next thought after the "aquarium" ending of my chant still had to be pure. So if after this little chant, including the aquarium reference, I thought something along the lines of "I'm with Satan," I had to expand on the prayer. Then it became "Sorry God, sorry God, sorry God, I love Jesus, I have seen an aquarium before today." (Notice the number 3's influence again.) The chant had various stages and expansions that I don't recall entirely. If I had a bad thought during my mental ritual, it would continue to grow. At its longest, it would include things like "I try to be a good person, I want to be with you forever, I try not to hurt people . . ." and would take me a good twenty or thirty seconds to say in my mind. I believe that extremely blasphemous thoughts or looking at something "Satanic" warranted an automatic "big sorry God"—this longest mental apology.

So I would go through my day and become upset and worried about the fact that when I got home, I had to say a group of "big sorry God's" in my mind. It wasn't devoting the time to say things in my mind that upset me; it was the potential for blasphemous thoughts during the chants. One Friday night, I was at an arcade for a friend's birthday party. The whole night was ruined for me because all I could think about was the fact that when I got home, I had to say thirteen "big sorry God's" in my mind. And I was worried that if I had an impure thought during my chants, the number would continue grow beyond thirteen. Obviously the whole thing was a game I invented to torture myself. Nowhere in the Bible does it state you have to pray to God about aquariums when you see strange symbols. I could have enjoyed a fun birthday party with friends, but instead, I had to ruin it for myself. I could have enjoyed life in general a lot more if I didn't give any thought to praying to God strangely and profusely throughout the day.

It wasn't just all about stress and chants in fifth grade. For some reason, this was my most rebellious grade-school year. Maybe I just had a strict teacher. I got four whole detentions throughout the school year. The first for ding-dong ditching a fourth-grade classroom. Not that it had a doorbell, but knocking on the door and running into the boys' bathroom (their teacher was female). Another detention I got simply because I was sent into the hallway for talking or misbehaving three times. That was the rule of the classroom.

Detention number three was more of a misunderstanding than anything else. I don't remember the details about what was happening in class at the time, but our teacher, Mr. Baker, was writing things on the board based on what students were yelling out. He misheard a group of kids yelling something several times, but I thought he was just joking around, pretending that he couldn't hear them.

"Clean your ears out, dude," I suggested, thinking it was all in good fun.

"You've got a detention!" he screamed at me. Clearly, I thought I was Bart Simpson.

My final detention only existed because of a tattletaling boy named Mark, who was an interesting fellow. At one point during creative writing, Mr. Baker said to us, "So far, we've been writing a lot of fictional stories. But what is the one thing you know more about, compared anyone else in the world?" The answer was obviously supposed to be ourselves, but Mark raised his hand and proudly exclaimed, "Building stuff out of Legos, I'm awesome at that!" For some reason, he always felt the need to tell on misbehaving kids. So during the lunch recess hour, Stefan and I would sneak off the playground and wander around the school. We made a pretty fun game out of it. We would try and stay hidden and not be noticed by any teachers or staff in the building while all the kids were outside playing. For some reason, Mark felt the need to tell the playground supervisor what Stefan and I were up to, so we each got detentions for it.

During this school year, students were rewarded fake money for performing classroom jobs, excelling in schoolwork, or behaving well. At the end of each semester, Mr. Baker held an auction. We used our fake money to purchase things like homework passes, candy, and toys. Most kids bought nice little collections of assorted knickknacks. I earned plenty of money from my schoolwork, but also lost a lot due to all the troublemaking. So at the end of the year, when all the auction toys were laid out, all I could afford was a pencil. But damn it, it was a spectacular pencil. I actually used it to write this book.

CHAPTER 3

I Was a Teenage Obsessive Compulsive

It was the fall of 1990. The world was heartbroken as Milli Vanilli returned their Grammy, but somehow I managed to straddle my Huffy and pedal off to middle school with small trendy lines shaved into the sides of my head. My OCD continued take on new forms. I remember feeling as though certain people were strange, or maybe evil, and their stare could have an effect on me. My loser friends and I sat next to a group of eighth-grade punks in the cafeteria. If I felt one of them was looking at me for a long amount of time, I would put my hands together and quickly loop my arms to the back of my neck, then bring them back to my chest, in such a way that looked like I was maybe fixing my hair. I felt I was somehow breaking the "bad" guys' stare, and otherwise, his looking at me could have a negative effect on who I was. Did I ever do it in a way that my friends would notice so I would have to explain myself? No, of course not, because I didn't want to explain myself. So luckily, the OCD rules were set up in a way that I wouldn't have to divulge the details to my friends. Because the ridiculous OCD rules are decided by myself, not by magical forces.

Recently, I've been watching old home videos that I started filming at this point in my life. My parents got a video camera in 1991, then volleyball-playin' Amy graduated high school a few months later. That left both of my sisters post high school and out of the house, and myself still three years away from running track in high school. Long story short, my parents didn't tape much of anything, so the camcorder basically became a toy for myself and my friends. Starting little movies about monsters or robbers that we never finished, or maybe taping ourselves playing basketball to watch our wicked awesome moves in slow motion. Watching myself on tape years later, I can see many instances of obsessive compulsive behaviors.

During the summer of '91, I was making a fake news broadcast with Matt. I was behind the desk (pool table), acting like a hyper little boy, reporting fake stories, traffic, and weather reports. At one point, I said, "I'm psychotic weatherman." Then immediately had to follow it up with "I'm not a weatherman" in a serious voice. This stemmed from my anxiety over a couple of things.

I had an unreasonable fear of tornadoes at this point in my life. Weather was especially violent in the Chicago land area in the spring of '91. It seemed as though we had thunderstorms and tornado warnings every other day. There was a powerful and deadly tornado in Plainfield, Illinois, around this time, and that contributed to my anxiety. So I felt as though I had to say "I'm not a weatherman" to somehow protect myself from bad weather. I don't know, maybe I didn't want the forces that controlled tornadoes to think I took severe weather lightly. I wanted to distract myself from the subconscious fears the term "weatherman" brought up for me.

I also was stressed over using the word "psychotic." Keeping my mind intelligent or sane has always been a fear of mine and something that had a huge influence on OCD. I felt as though I had to cancel out "psychotic" so I wouldn't become crazy. (I know, technically, I only said that I wasn't a weatherman, but somehow that counted as a twofer.)

In another video recorded in my backyard, I was acting silly and said the nonsense word "zabian" then immediately followed it up with "I don't love it." I don't know, "zabian" sounded like some kind of demonic name to me, so I had to let magical forces know that I didn't say "zabian" out of some kind of love or worship of the demon Zabian, in case there was one.

For some reason, at one point we started putting the camcorder on my dad's desk in my basement and filmed ourselves playing ping pong on the pool table. Exciting stuff, I know. If you want to buy a copy, just let me know. I saw myself acting out a lot of compulsions when I watched this. Mostly defusing negative energy off myself by doing things like jumping up and touching the ceiling. Actually, this led to one of the funniest moments of footage. My ball-tossing, ceiling-slap hopping got out of hand, and I dropped a paddle and said "shit!" loudly. At which point my mom yelled angrily from upstairs, "Jon! Stop that!" So you need to stop OCD'ing, pilgrim, or you're liable to be reprimanded for using a mouth of potty.

And lastly, at the end of a videotaped basketball game, I noticed another example of worrying that my spoken words could have serious consequences. It was right before the Gordons moved to California. I knew it would be the last time we were taped together, at least for a year, when they might come back to visit during the summer. I stopped recording when we were done playing, and a few seconds later, I started again. This was because I got a bad feeling when I stopped recording. I the said the word "good" and turned it off again, this time permanently. I felt if things were "off" the last time we recorded ourselves together, they would be "off" for an entire year until we were able to be filmed together again.

Here's what was really going on with this bad feeling. I was thinking about the future, thinking about the fact that they were moving, and I wanted to distract myself from that. I was upset that they were moving, and I was worried about how that might affect my social life, so I defused those feelings by saying "good," as though somehow, superstitiously, that would make everything I was worrying about okay. As I stated in the strategies, this is a huge part of OCD—rituals to distract yourself from subconscious worries, and defusing bad feelings through superstition.

I have a few last OCD-related memories from the middle-school years. At one point in seventh grade, I was playing darts with Lori in our basement. Before my turn, I sometimes touched the darts to the ground to defuse anxious feelings. She asked, "Why do you keep touching the ground? What are you, in leagues with Satan?" And I simply replied with a little evil smile, just joking around. You better believe I was praying profusely after the game. ("I didn't mean to imply that I'm with the devil, I'm sorry! I was just joking around!")

I have a final middle-school story that goes along with the theme of messing with people. During the summer after seventh grade, I had the house to myself for a couple hours every Thursday afternoon when my mom went grocery shopping (sticking to her daily/weekly routine, another OCD trait). I came up with a prank that just shows how much I was into ghosts and the unexplained. Using a little boom box, I recorded a short tape of strange noises. Toys banging around, strange music from my aforementioned Casio SK-1 Sampling Keyboard, dishes clanging, and a few seconds of random television noise.

While my mom was at the store, I put the tape into the cassette player in our kitchen and made sure that Matt and I were hanging out in my backyard. Soon enough, Matt would hear strange noises from my vacant house, and I would play along, acting as though I had no idea what they were. The tape worked out nicely in that Matt would be up against the back door trying to hear more muffled sounds, and one of the louder crashes would chime in, sending Matt running for dear life through my backyard. I think it even worked out perfectly once, when one of us said, "If that's a ghost in there, start playing the piano music now," and a second later, it just happened to be the keyboard section of the tape. Eventually, I let him know what was going on. But there's yet another example of me messing with the younger kids in the neighborhood and my obsession with the unexplained.

When I got to freshman year of high school, OCD became more powerful than ever before. It was similar to what happened to me in fifth grade; it was a stressful time for me. I was suddenly in high school. Four years of harder classes, driving, girls/dating/sex being an issue, trying to decide what to do post graduation, all that crap. I started with a second mind chant that reflected my main worries at the time. It went along the lines of:

"I go to heaven not hell in fifty-five years, and I'm cool and popular on this Earth, there's no nuclear war until the year 2085 and . . ."

Now let me elaborate. I always had to make sure that what I was saying in my chants was crystal clear for the magical forces listening to them. I added "not hell" to clear up any kind of confusion there. I wanted it to be clear I was talking about the afterlife, not some small town in western America called Heaven. "On this Earth," just in case God thought I wanted to be cool and popular in heaven, after death. I don't remember if I actually said "2085," but it was some year around there for sure. Which is interesting and very selfish on my part. I guess I wanted to make sure I would be dead, even if I lived an exceptionally long life. But apparently, I didn't care about anyone else. Possible children or grandchildren, nieces, nephews, every other living person on the planet—looks like my attitude was to let them all burn in a nuclear fire, as long as I wasn't there to experience it. Couldn't I have just thought "there's never a nuclear war"? Maybe I thought that would be asking for too much, as though nuclear war was inevitable, and putting it off until 2085 was already asking a lot. And why fifty-five years? I was only fourteen, that would have made my death at age sixty-nine. Seems like I should have gone with sixty-five years, at least. The end of the chant, "and . . . . ," there was usually something tacked on that reflected something in the immediate future I was worried about, as opposed to general anxieties about nuclear war and the afterlife. For example, it would end "there's no nuclear war until 2085, and I do good on the math test Friday."

So I would go though the day, saying this is my mind multiple times. (Oh, and by the way, I couldn't have been farther from cool and popular in high school. So it doesn't work—OCD is fake. And I'm very embarrassed to admit that being "cool and popular" was so important to me. Not sure I could tell you exactly why that was.) This chant stressed me out so much that I think I may have even played around with it at one point to prove it wasn't affecting my life. One day I added "And when I get home tonight, our house will have been robbed," and of course, that never happened. But that wasn't good enough to disprove anything. I had to keep doing it. Clearly I knew the chants were futile if I threw in nonsense about our house being robbed, but because of the way my brain is wired, that didn't stop me from having to recite them.

In my freshman year math class, I felt I had to touch an area on the floor near my desk every once in a while. And of course, it was a class I was having difficulty with, so I was stressed at the time. I would touch an area under the desk of the kid next to me, as though I was picking up a pencil. He gave me some strange looks at times, which is probably why I felt as though I had to keep doing it. Just torturing myself into looking like some floor-touching fool to the guy next to me. (I sat in the back row. I'm sure if I had sat somewhere up front, the magical OCD rules would have been different as to spare me from looking foolish to those behind me. What a coincidence.)

One OCD ritual involving chewing gum comes to mind because I recall John asking me why I was doing it. I would periodically take the gum out of my mouth and hold it next my face, then resume chewing. Sometimes I would take it out of my mouth, jump up and touch the ceiling, then start chewing it again. Why was I doing this? I don't know; I had to defuse the negative energy off my gum to make sure the future was good. Had to keep those pesky demons out of myself.

Looking at certain areas in my line of sight and blinking was another one. Same kind of defusing negative energy or spirits. I remember being out for dinner at Pizza Hut with my dad, and he asked if there was something wrong with my eyes. Of course I said no and left it at that. What was I going to say? Just like I offered John no explanation for the chewing gum shenanigans.

This was also something I found myself doing right before the gun went off at the beginning of track races. As we lined up and the starter was about to shoot his gun, I felt the need to look off to the side of the track and blink. Looking back on this now, of course it was because I had a lot of anxiety about how I was going to perform. And I dealt with this anxiety by doing strange things with my eyes, as though that would make me run well. Obviously there's no real connection; it was just how I dealt with my apprehension. I think it's safe to say many athletes have rituals and superstitions that could definitely be considered forms of OCD. The Boston Red Sox's Wade Boggs was an incredibly superstitious athlete. He had to eat chicken before every game, always take 150 ground balls during infield practice, enter the batting cage at exactly 5:17, and often tap his glove two or three times before pitches. Just another example of why you shouldn't be ashamed of your bizarre thoughts. I mean, in spite of his loony rituals, he earned a spot in the Baseball Hall of Fame as well as a guest appearance on *Cheers* in which he was depantsed.

Which brings me to a story about the power of the mind. We've all heard the stories of the parent that can suddenly lift a car to save his or her child. I think we can all relate to the sense of confidence and success that follows truly believing in yourself. This causes a problem with OCD; things feel very real when you believe in them. It's easy to feel like you're suddenly a different person if you really believe you might be. A few stories that apply from my life have to do with running. Freshman year, I was a pretty crappy runner. At the end of the season, we had our conference meet against the eight big schools in our county, and Wheaton North, my school, was expected to win (on the varsity level anyway). I was slated to run the mile, and all day, I psyched myself up for the race. Not that my performance in the freshman/sophomore mile would affect the varsity standing, but it was still the biggest meet I had ever been a part of. All day I concentrated on running well, and during the race, I constantly told myself I had to go all out because it was such an important race. I ended up beating my personal record by around thirty seconds, which is quite a difference for the mile, and finished with one of the fastest mile times out of all underclassmen on my team.

Likewise, during my junior year cross-country season, a fellow runner gave a quick lecture to the team about "gut breathing." He said the key to performing well was to take the time before a race to relax, close your eyes, and slowly breathe deeply from your stomach as opposed to your lungs. While doing this, you would also picture in your mind exactly what you wanted to accomplish. One morning before a race that I thought I could perform quite well in, I tried his recommended technique. During the bus ride and before the race, I closed my eyes, breathed deeply, and imagined myself in detail leading the pack early on and crossing the finish line in first. Sure enough, I ended up beating all two hundred or so runners by a good twenty seconds. Now believe me, I'm not trying to brag about some fast race fourteen years ago. I'm just trying to illustrate the fact that the mind can be a very powerful thing. When you try to ignore your compulsions, it's going to feel like you're different or that something bad is going to happen in your future, but you have to tell yourself it isn't real; your mind is just making it feel real.

Freshman year, I also seemed to have a feeling that intervals of time actually existed as if they were something to enter. Let me explain. On New Years Eve '93, I was sleeping over at the Gordons with E. J. As soon as the clock struck twelve, I had to immediately think superstitious thoughts in my mind. Probably the same kinds of things from my chant—going to heaven, being cool, nuclear war, whatever else I may have been worrying about at the time. I felt as though if I said positive things about myself and the future in my mind right when I was officially entering 1994, it would be a good year. Most people probably have anxieties about the upcoming year—thinking about what's going to happen, wondering what things will be like the following New Year's Eve. But of course, I had to magically seal my fate.

At times, my compulsions had a religious theme that almost makes sense. Or they're easier to explain than something like defusing demons off my gum anyway. Halfway through freshman year was when I found out the Gordons might be moving to California. It wasn't official until maybe May. So of course, I was worried that my best friends/almost entire social life was going to be two thousand miles away all of the sudden. At this point in my life, my trio of friends and I were into silly pranks, like ding-dong ditching and ordering pizzas for people. One night, I was deciding whether or not I wanted to order a pizza for my neighbors, and I got a bad feeling about it. It somehow turned into "if I order the pizza, the Gordons will, in fact, move to California." That sounds a little superstitious, but there's also a factor of punishment. As though if I were doing bad things, God would punish me. (I mean, can you imagine how angry God gets when someone orders a pizza for a neighbor for no reason? I probably would have been struck by lightning!)

This also comes back to thinking about OCD on a bigger scale, and how people with the disorder feel like they can control such life-altering events. Maybe we don't necessarily believe we have that kind of power, but it at least gives us a sense of comfort if we act like we can control the uncontrollable. As if my daily actions would determine the events at the company where Mr. Gordon worked or have some kind of influence over their decision to move. And I more or less believed that, because I did end up ordering that pizza. So let me just say—that's right, Eggleston family, it was I who ordered a pizza for you in January of 1994! What are you gonna do about it?!

We had some pretty interesting pranks over the years. At one point, Matt and I would stand at a three-way intersection underneath a streetlight near his house. When a car approached from a block or two away, we would pretend to light a stick of dynamite (stuffed cardboard paper towel tube) then run and hide. I don't think drivers ever had much of a reaction, except once when it happened to be a cop, who stopped and flashed a search light around to see what was going on. ("Oh my god, it's a cop . . . . go, JUST GO!") Remember the movie *The Good Son*, when Macaulay Culkin threw a dummy off an overpass and caused a massive car pileup? We made our own dummy out of my old clothes, stuffed with leaves and sewn by my mother. I think we told her it was a scarecrow for Halloween, which was right around the corner. We left it off to the side of the street at night in front of the Gordons house. Cars always slowed almost to a stop, realized it was a dummy, then drove off. Until one day, when someone stopped, took the dummy into their car, and drove away (because hey, free dummy).

The most memorable ding-dong ditching incident was a night when I rang someone's doorbell, then came back for seconds a few minutes later. When I was a few steps away from the door, a woman whispered from a window, "What do you want?" I froze, then turned around and started running as she screamed "Get out of here you little jerk!" like she wanted to kill me. I sprinted for probably two hundred meters with a look on my face that probably resembled a rabbit trying to outrun a wolf.

My favorite ding-dong ditching story is one that I wasn't involved with, but heard about from Matt after he moved. Apparently, a group of little boy ding-dongers had a rule that if they got caught, they were to pretend they needed to borrow a cup of sugar. So Matt's friend rang a doorbell, then tried to sprint away but fell down the stairs. He ended up lying on the ground crying because he was hurt. When the resident opened the door, the boy asked between sobs, "Can I borrow a cup of sugar?"

So freshman year came to an end, and the Gordons shipped out to the West Coast. I recall that on the last day of school freshman year, a half day, I came home to have the house to myself. A few days earlier, a large wooden sign announced "It's a boy!" in the front yard across the street from ours. It was the Murrays' house, actually, but the Murrays had moved out, and a new family was living there. Apparently, this family had some relatives in town for the arrival of the baby boy. On this particular afternoon, one of them, a girl—I would guess was about nineteen at the time—decided to sunbathe in their front yard. She was an extremely busty girl, sporting a small white bikini and clearly showing off her body for the entire neighborhood.

In my room, I had a miniature telescope that had been a free gift for subscribing to some scientific magazine several years earlier. It had a little tripod and was probably eighteen inches at the most when completely stretched out. So I did what any hormone-filled fifteen-year-old dork would have done—set up the telescope on the couch next to me so that when I peered through the viewfinder, the entire circle was taken up by her enormous chest. This would have been a funny sight for a family member to walk in on. I mean, imagine someone looking into a miniature telescope and jacking off.

Along similar lines, at one point sophomore year, I was watching newly released *Speed* on VHS in my basement with my friend Phil. During the elevator rescue scene, there is of course a gratuitous shot of a woman's underwear as her miniskirt is accidentally lifted up by Jeff Daniels. Phil told me to rewind this shot for a second viewing. (I know, but we were fifteen, and he wasn't even allowed to watch R-rated movies. Plus, the Internet wasn't mainstream yet.) After I did, I of course got a bad feeling and felt as though I had to do it again. This is because I would look like a weirdo pervert rewinding the shot multiple times, so I was just torturing myself. A few seconds passed as I tried to ignore my uneasy feeling, and a few more people were rescued from the doomed elevator until I finally mumbled something about watching it one more time, and rewind all the way back to that stupid shot. "What's wrong with you?" Phil asked, and that's exactly what I was afraid of—OCD torturing me into doing something that made me look like some freak that just *had* to see a quick shot of a thong bottom again.

Another compulsion around this time actually led to the destruction of a piece of furniture. It may have been the first time OCD had an actual negative impact on my life, besides stress and performing odd behaviors. Amy was home for Christmas break, and one night, she was playing some Super Nintendo in my room while I was sitting on the bed behind her. Suddenly, I had to jump up and touch the ceiling to defuse a bad feeling. I pretty much just landed ass first on my bed on the way down. Unfortunately, I was too old and big to do such a thing. The wooden bed frame broke, and the mattress fell halfway to the floor, no longer supported.

This is a pretty amusing thing for me to picture now. A fifteen-year-old jumping on his bed, which he's way too old to be doing in the first place. So the bed frame breaks, all because he had to touch the ceiling to make the future better. Of course, when I was asked what happened, I said I just sat down way too fast.

Something interesting happens in my life at this point. When I look back and try and remember OCD examples from my last couple of years of high school and even my freshman year of college, there pretty much aren't any. OCD seemed to be a childhood problem, then went away when I was sixteen or so, then came back with a vengeance in my early twenties. From what I've read, OCD becoming a significant problem in your early twenties is pretty common. But it does seem a little backwards to me. Freshman year of high school can be stressful because it's new, but it seems like junior and senior years would be even worse. You're suddenly pretty much a legal adult, trying to figure out what to do after high school and, in a lot of cases, getting ready to move out of the house or even the state. For whatever reason, my disorder kind of took a break for a few years once I was done growing. So to fill the void, the following chapter is nothing but entertaining or amusing stories from those few years of my life when it went away. If you are only looking for OCD advice or analysis, you'd be better off just skipping to chapter 5, where it becomes a significant problem.

CHAPTER 4

The Adventures of Long-Distance Running Dorks

Seriously, this is nothing but goofy stories. No mention of OCD until chapter 5. Just a warning.

An interesting tradition we had on the cross-country team was the practice of toileting. Some runners a few years ahead of me started it. Throughout the season, each team member would receive a knock on their door and an actual toilet on their doorstep late at night. It often had fire emerging from it, and their front yard would be toilet papered. It was then that runner's responsibility to pass the toilet on to a different team member who had yet to be toileted, until it had been received by the entire team. In addition to toilet paper and fire, at times, yards might be vandalized with car tires, street barricades, gourds, cat food, fish, shaving cream, large objects from neighbor's discarded trash, or mayonnaise.

One particular toileting adventure, Mark (building stuff out of Legos), myself, and a few other runners stopped at the local grocery store to stock up on vandalism supplies. Mark returned to the car with a couple handfuls of random items.

"Check it out, all this stuff was free!" he proudly informed us, laying a pile of panty hose and other cheap things in the car. "They were in a clearance bin, the price tags all say 'zero dollars, zero cents'!" He then proceeded to unwrap a pair of panty hose and insert his head into them, like a criminal. At which point, an employee knocked on my car window.

"Um, that stuff isn't free," she informed him. Embarrassed, he returned the items to the store and was forced to purchase the pair of panty hose that his head had been inside of.

And a memory that involves both Mark and my friend Eric is an example of me recruiting a friend to mess with people. One Saturday night, Eric and I knew that Mark was home alone. We snuck into his back door and started spying on him as he watched television in the living room. Eventually we made it upstairs and started blasting the stereo to freak him out. He had absolutely no reaction to this. (He would tell us later that he thought he hadn't heard his sister come home, and she was playing music loudly in her room.) Next we went into his basement to play with the fuse box. He had a small crawl space that I stood next to as Eric shut off various fuses—my job was to let him know when the sound of the television vanished, as I was pretty much standing right underneath the living room. When he got to maybe the third fuse, the TV was shut off. I told Eric he got the right one, and we both hid in the crawl space. Mark got on the phone with the electric company but then realized half of his house had power, and his neighbors' windows were still shining brightly. He slowly came downstairs and opened the door to the crawl space wielding a butcher knife. Luckily, no one was maimed.

As the Internet became increasing popular in the late '90s, I had a new means of screwing with people. Senior year, I began talking to my friend Chris online under a screen name he wasn't familiar with. Chris was a fellow runner, and a year younger than me. I pretended to be a girl from St. Charles, a neighboring city of Wheaton. I kept up the charade for several weeks. For a while, I just toyed around to see what kinds of things he would say to some random girl online. Eventually, I told him that I ran into a friend of his in a chat room, Jon Davis (myself), and we had met in real life. So then I just kind of talked about Jon Davis to see what Chris thought about me. For example, "Jessica" (that was the fake name I went by) asked Chris if Jon was a good dancer after a Wheaton North dance. Chris's response was "Fuck no! He needs to loosen up."

It was all just too fun, so I started adding to it. After a month or so, Jessica was acting very upset one night. She told Chris something along the lines of "Remember how I told you I met your friend Jon? Well, we did more than just meet. We actually had sex on New Year's Eve. And now I'm pregnant."

Chris continued to eat the whole story up. It was amusing for me to talk to him as Jessica online after that. He told her, "We were all goofing around at practice today, and Jon was acting funny and happy. I was looking at him, and I was just sad. I mean, he has no idea he got you pregnant." After a few days, I confessed my true identity. ("You douche bag! I can't believe that was you saying all that crap!")

Lunch was always an amusing time senior year. I brought a group of maybe five friends home every day. There wasn't enough room for all of them in the Chevy Beretta, so one of them rode in the trunk. It was very amusing for my neighbor to see my car pull into our driveway every afternoon, at which point the trunk would pop open and a teenage boy (who just happened to be about the same size as the trunk itself) would crawl out. We then all headed to my basement to watch twenty minute segments of one of my '80s or '90s movies on VHS for a week until we had completed it (our lunch breaks were pretty short). When it was time to watch *Who Framed Roger Rabbit?* we tried to determine the validity of the rumor about animators slipping in a quick peek at Jessica Rabbit's pubic hair. During the scene in question, Jessica flies from Benny the Cab in her dress, and her legs are facing the viewer for half a second. It was hard to tell, so we paused it. The TV in our basement was fairly small, so one (quite possibly two) of my friends got on their hands and knees in front of it. At which point, my mom walked in to find the TV paused on a cartoon character with her legs spread, with two seventeen-year-old boys on their hands and knees just inches away from the screen. She simply said, "I don't even want to know," and left the room.

That certainly wasn't the only time my mom walked in on us acting like idiots. We sometimes made stupid little home videos, like I had done with the Gordons and E. J. years earlier. During one, someone was talking to the camera, and my friend Shane decided to sneak around the corner behind him. He then mooned the camera a few times. My mom happened to walk in while we were watching this video during lunch and asked what it was.

"Just . . . . a movie we made," I told her.

"Something about a butt?" she teased. That was a little awkward.

My other friend Pat would immediately go straight to the basement computer, sign on to America Online, and try to get as many porn pictures as he could in "pic" chat rooms. At one point, he discovered a picture of a hideous sexual act, which literally sent multiple friends of mine screaming and running from the room.

On the drive to and from my house, I would drive strangely and recklessly, but not in a dangerous kind of way. Speeding, drifting into other lanes, running stop signs. Just showing off I guess, trying to be funny. I think maybe I was hoping some girls from school would see me driving strangely, and it would turn them on so much that they would have sex with me. At one point, I was pulled over by a cop when I got back to the school parking lot. He informed me that based on all the little laws I broke while I was driving, he could fine me around $300 and revoke my license. But for some reason, he just let me go without a warning.

A few months later, I had another run-in with the law, but this time, I wasn't so lucky. At one point, Pat and I bought a couple small BB guns. They were black handguns that looked somewhat like real .45s. Once we started firing them, we found out that they were exceptionally weak. Firing a shot across my backyard, the BB would literally be on the ground twenty feet away from me. At one point, I held the gun up against an empty soda can and fired, and it wasn't even dented.

Right after graduation, Pat took a trip to Wisconsin with his family and borrowed my gun for some reason. A week later, he and Shane picked me up on a Saturday night to go to a movie. Pat returned my gun to me in the car and, for some reason, brought his own rifle BB gun that was actually powerful. On the way to the movie, I shot a stop sign and a speed limit sign as we drove past them on residential streets. No cars were around, and I'm not sure I even stuck my gun out of the car. At an intersection a few blocks from the movie, Pat, in the passenger seat, tried to shoot at a streetlight. But even then, it didn't seem like there were any witnesses around to see it.

So we got to the movie theater, and the film we wanted to see was sold out. We started driving back through the parking lot the way we came. We turned a few corners, and a cop passed drove passed us, looking at us suspiciously. We didn't think much of it as we made our way through the many connected parking lots.

Suddenly, after turning a corner, two police cars stopped in front of us, blocking our path. Three more pulled up behind us.

"Driver of the vehicle—turn off the car and throw the keys out the window," a voice on a bullhorn commanded from behind us. Shane did so, and then he was instructed to exit the vehicle with his hands in the air.

As he walked away from the car and was instructed to lie on the ground facedown and put his hands behind his back to be handcuffed, he said "Fuck you, Pat," assuming the reason this was all going down was Pat's sniper shot at the light.

"Shut the fuck up!" a police officer yelled back.

It was then Pat's turn to do the same thing. I of course was next, and as I made my walk of shame, I could see that several police officers had their guns drawn and pointed at me, crouching behind their car doors, ready to take me out if I tried to shoot at them.

Apparently what had happened was someone called the police with a bullshit story about three kids driving around shooting at people. This exaggerating douche bag of a citizen even said that we aimed our guns at someone and they ducked in terror. This was a complete and udder lie. The cops, after hearing this story, didn't know what was going on with us exactly. For all they knew, the guns were real. So they showed up in full force and used the same tactics they would have if we were actual drive-by murderers.

We were all taken to the police stations in separate squad cars, led into separate interrogation rooms, stripped of our shoes and belts, and told our story to the investigating officers in turn. In the end, I had to go to court and pay two $75 tickets. One for discharging a gun in Wheaton, and one for something along the lines of endangering or frightening the public.

When I got to college, one of my stupid little jokes backfired on me. This also involved Pat. He visited me in my dorm with a group of friends when I was a freshman and he was in his last year of high school. For some reason, his glasses ended up in the urinal of the bathroom that was directly across from my room. I think they were broken, and he thought it would be funny to leave them in the urinal; I don't remember exactly. After the group went back to Wheaton, I wrote on the marker board on our door: "Missing: one pair of glasses. If found, please return to me immediately." So anyone that peed would pee all over the glasses, wondering what they were doing there, then exit the bathroom and read our message.

After a day or so, the cleaning crew removed the glasses from the urinal and put them on the shelf over the sinks. After a few hours, I got a knock on my door from someone who was just seeing the glasses and message for the first time.

"Here, they were right in the bathroom," he informed me, previously urine-soaked glasses in hand.

"Oh . . . . thanks," I said, reluctantly taking the glasses that had been peed on by thirty guys.

And of course, with college comes funny drinking stories. Remember when you first started getting drunk and you were living with your parents, and sometimes you had to talk to them at night and pretend you were sober? The first time this happened to me, I had a conversation with my mom for a few minutes returning home before I went to bed. Afterwards I felt I put on a pretty good show acting sober. The next morning, she mentioned something about me being drunk the night before.

"How'd you know that?!" I was shocked.

"Because when we talked last night, you couldn't form a coherent sentence."

Shane was an interesting drunk. He was funny and entertaining to begin with, but once he had several Jack and Cokes in him, he put on quite a show. One night, after a good bit of drinking, we found ourselves at a Taco Bell. Shane stood on top of a table and started pushing up the ceiling tiles. The people working behind the counter asked what he was doing, and he told them he was "looking for napkins." Oddly enough, their response to this was to happily whip out a fat stack of napkins and say, "We keep them back here."

On a different occasion, one of the first times he was drunk, several people were passed out in my dorm room late at night, with the exception of myself and my roommate. Shane, who had been silent and motionless for several minutes, suddenly sat up, looked more towards the door than at any actual person, and said, "Quit masturbating, fat tits!" He then laid back down and went to sleep. He had absolutely no recollection of saying this the next day. And that was just the beginning. Several years later, he attended a party for several hours with his testicles hanging out of his fly. If anyone pointed it out to him, he told them they were a new pair of pants, and he hadn't figured out how to wear them yet.

I've always been a big wuss about taking shots. Sometimes, if I'm already very drunk, a shot of hard liquor causes me to throw up. One night, when I was at a bar with a few friends, the bartender gave us a shot of Wild Turkey. I don't even remember why exactly; I'm sure none of us ordered it. I gave it a try, but after it was in my mouth for a few seconds, I was afraid swallowing it would have disastrous consequences, so I spit it back into the shot glass and put it on the bar.

"You guys don't want this?" the bartender asked when he noticed it was back on the bar. Before we could stop him, he was offering it to a group of people at the end of the bar. Some random girl ended up downing it. I guess she was too drunk to wonder why it was warm.

The best drinking story I have took place at Chris's high school graduation party. I drank probably ten to twelve beers, so eventually I was completely wasted. As soon as I started feeling sick, I wanted to lie down by myself somewhere. In my drunken state, the best place I could think of was atop a small shed in his backyard. I laid there staring at the stars, for some reason contemplating whether or not I believed in God. Every once in a while, I could hear a male party attendant peeing on the ground near me, unaware of my presence. The next day, everyone was surprised that I actually laid on top of this shed without it collapsing, and when I took a sober look at it, I was too. It looked like a strong breeze would knock it down.

After several minutes on the rickety roof, I joined a group of people sitting around a fire pit. But I felt as though I might be sick soon, so I ventured into the house for a place to lie down. There were people on the main floors and speakers blaring music in Chris's room, so I went to the top level and found a bathroom. I figured no one would be using it since there were other bathrooms closer to the party. So I laid in the bathtub and closed the shower curtain with the light off and the bathroom door open.

For a few minutes, I laid there with my eyes closed as the room spun. But suddenly, someone came in to use the bathroom. My initial reaction was to quickly warn them of my presence, but I decided I'd be embarrassed to be found lying in the tub. So I decided to wait it out.

Unfortunately, I soon discovered why this person sought out such a secluded bathroom. The noises and the odor were too much for me, and there was nothing I could do but to get on my hand and knees and begin vomiting.

Of course, this turned out to be quite a shock to the person in the bathroom with me. A middle-aged woman's voice rang through the room, angrily asking something along the lines of "Are you fucking kidding me?!"

"BLAH! Sorry . . . . BLAH!" was my response.

It was very embarrassing for the both of us. I didn't know the woman, but I apologized profusely to her that night and the following day.

CHAPTER 5

Her Death Turns OCD into a Monster

December of 1998 is the first time I remember OCD coming back into my life after early high school. The end of my first semester, sophomore year of college. I was worried about grades, and it was finals week. I felt I had done well on a few exams, and I was nervous about keeping that trend going. I was suddenly repeating little everyday actions to make sure I kept doing well on my finals. At the time, I probably thought to myself, "This is interesting, I haven't done this superstitious stuff since I was a kid." But it still barely existed; I can't think of any examples for another year.

I will quickly throw in story number one of two about why you shouldn't do drugs. It took place around this time. Chris and I spent a lot of time with our friend from high school, Jeff. He was half a hippie and smoked marijuana on a regular basis. One night when we were playing pool at a bar, two very muscular trashy-looking gentlemen asked Jeff if he had any weed. He told them he did, but not on him. They informed him that they were convicts, recently out of prison, and that he had to go back to his dorm and bring his weed to the bar. The deal was they would keep Chris and I hostage, more or less, to make sure Jeff came back.

Were they really convicts? I don't know; they looked like they certainly could have been. While Jeff was making his trip, they tried to intimidate us by saying things like "I hope your friend comes back. We just got out of prison, and we're not afraid to go back, if you know what I mean." Not that this was necessarily that big of a deal. In the end, Jeff came back, and they let us go. It just seems worth mentioning.

In the year 2000, the summer before my senior year, OCD started getting a little worse. I was definitely more stressed in life and worried about the future. I only had one year of school left and pretty much no idea what I was going to do after graduation. I majored in English, simply because it was what I enjoyed most in school and I liked writing. I didn't exactly have any jobs lined up.

My jaw does this thing where it kind of mildly dislocates if I open my mouth as wide as I can. Nothing serious, just kind of an odd feeling that I try to avoid. It used to happen when I yawned at times. Not long before senior year began, I felt the need to do it repeatedly, until I felt good about the future. This is another example of forcing myself to do something I didn't want to do. It seemed unnatural to me that my jaw was sliding out of place, and I worried that if I did it a lot, it might lock or cause some kind of damage. So of course, I would get bad feelings about it, forcing myself to repeat it and flirt with the possibility of damaging my jaw.

My second antidrug story is my one experience with ecstasy. Technically, I did it twice. But it was two nights in a row, and night number two was terrible. Two nights before I moved into an apartment in Champaign with Chris senior year, I took an ecstasy pill with a couple friends. As soon as it kicked in, I enjoyed the way it made me feel—happy, with a sensitive body. We went downtown Chicago to a club for a while and came back home. My friend gave me a few more pills to keep.

The following night, I went on a date, and because of the way I had reacted to it the night before, I thought it was a perfect time to take another tablet. I figured it would make me more relaxed and confident, and if anything physical happened, it would enhance that. About half an hour after I took it, as I was driving to meet her, I suddenly got an extremely bad migraine. It was so painful that I very seriously considered driving to an emergency room and telling them that I had just taken ecstasy and was in excruciating pain. I bought Tylenol and water at a gas station, but it barely helped the situation. I cancelled the date, headed home, and tried drinking water as I drove. I knew you're supposed to stay hydrated with ecstasy, but I was in so much pain that my body just rejected it. I ended up vomiting a little into a plastic bag multiple times on the drive home.

And this headache plagued me for a couple weeks. It wasn't necessarily constantly there, but any time I exerted myself physically at all—such as walking up several flights of stairs—it would come back. If I had an orgasm, it would come back throbbing. So, don't do ecstasy, kids. Those chemicals mess with your brain.

As the school year started, I found myself practicing compulsions more than I had in years. One random example I can think of is deciding which chip or Cheeto should be my last to eat. As I was finishing my snack, I would eat a "last" chip until I felt good about the future. At one point, I even said something along the lines of "There, that one will make my future good" when Chris was there, just to see if I would get any kind of reaction. He probably just thought I was trying to be a weirdo.

One night in my room, I was standing up with my hand on the wall, and as I leaned away and removed my hand, there was a slight knocking from the inner wall. I hit the same spot a few times, and the knocking was even louder. Apparently, there was something in the inner wall that must have been hanging up against my bedroom wall, and when I pushed on it, it would swing away and hit my wall a few times before resting in place. I don't know much about construction, but this seemed pretty odd to me. I'm guessing it was a mistake, a loose piece of wood left hanging by a nail, perhaps. I got a very uneasy feeling about the future and had to repeat it several times before feeling somewhat "good" about things. I don't know why exactly this noise seemed so odd to me and caused a lot of stress and repeats. I think it was just a sign that I was getting older and more anxious about life.

As 2001 rolled around, OCD continued to grow stronger. One night, I got a bad feeling when I turned my computer off before bed. I worried about it as I tried to fall asleep, and it bothered me enough that I actually got out of bed, turned the computer back on, only to shut it down in order to defuse my anxiety. This was a level of OCD I hadn't seen in years. It's one thing to repeat little quick actions like jaw opening and chip eating, but I actually waited a good fifteen minutes, got back out of bed, and turned a computer on just to turn it off. I knew the whole time that what I was doing was illogical, and if someone could see me, I wouldn't be able to offer a reasonable explanation for what I was doing. But because I was about to enter the "real world," my compulsions became more involved to counter with my increased level of anxiety about life.

On a different night when I went to bed, I felt the compulsion to turn the volume on my clock radio extremely high for a second. Chris and his girlfriend had just gone to bed in his room across the hall. So of course, I felt the need to turn the volume up exceptionally loud several times, until I felt good about things. This was because I knew they could hear it, and they would wonder what I was doing. It took me a while to get a "good" feeling when I did it because I knew every time my alarm was blasting music for a split second, they would wonder what the hell I was doing. I'm sure the sudden and brief noise of the radio being at full blast gave me a natural anxious feeling as well, which didn't help.

It was around this point that I learned my mom was about to die from the cancer that had been diagnosed a few years earlier, and OCD took on a whole new form.

My stress level went through the roof as soon as I learned she probably had about two weeks left. I never had anyone close to me die, and suddenly, the person that raised me was going to be gone. This was the person I grew inside of, so I'm sure that brought up all kinds of subconscious thoughts about my own mortality. Also, she had a very strict Catholic upbringing that didn't sit well with her. She was outspoken about her disbelief in God. I remember her talking about some of the stories from the Old Testament of God's wrath or punishments, specifically the story of Abraham being asked to sacrifice his son. She didn't understand why anyone would worship a God like that. At this point in my life, I had a very black and white, good and evil, heaven and hell view of the world. So not only was I stressed about losing her, but part of me worried that she might be going to hell.

My compulsions got out of hand. She passed away on April 25, 2001. During the month of April, I drove home from school every weekend, and my sisters were back home from Colorado a lot of the time. One Friday night, I was in our basement putting sheets on the mattress of our fold-out couch. I got a bad feeling after I made the bed, as though I had to do it again. I tried to ignore it and went to bed. The next morning, it still bothered me. I knew OCD was evolving because it was the first time that a "bad" feeling actually made it through the night and lasted more than one day.

When I returned to school probably that same week, there was one night in particular when Chris had a friend over. They were in his room, and I was across the hall in mine with the door shut. I dropped a textbook on the floor; it was loud, and I immediately got a bad feeling. Probably related to my mom surviving as long as possible or going to heaven when she died. So I had to drop the book again. I knew that when I dropped it, Chris and his friend could hear it. Long story short, I ended up dropping it quite possibly a dozen times until I had a "good" feeling. Every time I dropped it, it made a loud noise, and I knew Chris and his friend would wonder what I was doing. Because I didn't want to keep doing it, my OCD made me keep doing it. I think after Chris's friend left he asked me about the whole ordeal, and it went something along the lines of:

Chris: What was all that banging before?
Me: Oh, just my book.
Chris: What were you doing with it?
Me: I just kept . . . . dropping it.
Chris: Um, okay . . . .

That was what I was afraid of, having to explain why I kept slamming it to the ground. It could have been something undetected by others, like tapping a pencil to a piece of paper. But darn it, that pesky OCD made it something that I would have to explain later. Because how was I supposed to respond to Chris? "Oh, I had to drop my Psych book on the ground the right amount of times for my mom to get into heaven"?

As she was about to die, the compulsions become stronger and more involved than ever before. One night at school, I returned from picking up something to eat, and I parked my car in a parking lot a few blocks away from our apartment. I had a bad feeling about the spot I parked in but tried to ignore it. I walked home, and I sat in my room stressed about it for a while, until I actually walked all the way back to the parking lot to switch spots. I knew it was getting out of control at this point. It was like the computer incident, but far worse.

After she died, I had a lot of problems with anxiety in general. Sleeping was hard for me. When I was about to fall asleep at night, I would have a panic attack and feel as if my heart was about to stop beating. Looking back now, I know I was just extremely afraid of death after having a real experience with it for the first time. I remember thinking that if someone could guarantee I would be alive and healthy in twelve hours, I would be able to sleep. When I began to feel relaxed as though I was about to fall asleep, I would have an irrational fear of dying in my sleep and my heart rate would go through the roof.

So as I was dealing with this new level of anxiety, of course my OCD got worse. There was an incident in June of 2001 involving a set of shelves. It was by far the worse thing I had ever dealt with as far as OCD is concerned. And at this point, I still didn't know I had OCD. I knew I had some strange, superstitious thoughts, and I had learned a little about OCD in school, but I wasn't necessarily convinced that it applied to me.

I moved back home from Champaign to the house I grew up in, now living with just my dad. I had a few final classes to take at the local community college to transfer to U of I and finish my degree. As I unpacked my things and put them away in my room, I got a bad feeling when I put a set of shelves into my closet. I think I moved them back out and in a few times, but I kept getting bad feelings and knew it would continue. Partially because it was somewhat of an effort, so I knew if I jinxed myself into getting a bad feeling, I'd have to do it all over again. But more importantly, I knew the shelves would remain in my closet for quite possibly several years. This has always been a theme with my OCD—permanence. For example, if I was going to bury something and leave it in the ground for ten years, I would be very likely to get a bad feeling and want to bury it all over again. I would feel as though if things were jinxed when I buried it, they would remain jinxed for all the years the item remained buried. Something like that would cause me a great deal more anxiety than a daily activity such as parking a car that would be moved the next day.

This characteristic of OCD is about dealing with my anxiety about the future. Maybe when I put the shelves in my closet, somewhere in my mind I thought "these will be here for years," and that immediately gave me a good deal of anxiety about my future. I always worry about the next few years of my life in terms of things such as money, occupation, health, and health of loved ones.

I should also add that at this point in my life, the OCD fears were specific. In the past, it had been a general bad feeling, but now there were a few key things I was worried about. The main ones were the following: my mom being in heaven, myself getting into heaven, being smart, and making enough money at whatever job I ended up having now that school was over. For example, I would enter a room and go through those four specific worries in my mind. I might feel good about everything except my mom being in heaven, so I would have to reenter the room to make sure she was in heaven. This is pretty funny for me to look back on now. If these magical rules worked this way, was she in hell at one point, and because I repeated some trivial action, she was transferred to heaven instead? That must have been pretty annoying for her being transferred back and forth between heaven and hell all day. I'm totally going to be grounded for a few weeks if I get to heaven.

So when I put these shelves into my bedroom closet, my specific worry was about my intelligence. I've worried a lot over the years about my level of intelligence. I have a pretty weird mind, smart in some ways and not so much in others. I wanted to be smart, and I thought that a lot in my life—such as how much money I made or how happy and successful I would be—depended on that. So basically, I felt like I was stupid because of the amount of times I put the shelves in my closet. I stopped doing it because I knew no matter how many times I put them back in there, I would get a bad feeling. Also, unintelligent is something I would settle for compared to damnation. So I tried to live with this feeling that I was suddenly a good deal less intelligent all of the sudden.

This proved to be damn near impossible. It's hard to explain exactly how I felt at this time, but just imagine if you truly believed that your IQ had magically gone down thirty-five points all of the sudden. I was in this strange, anxious mood all the time. I was extra nervous around people, feeling that my mind was suddenly not up to par. I had trouble remembering things or figuring things out simply because I believed the magic was real. It was almost as though I could physically feel something was wrong with my brain, as if some of it were missing or there was a slight feeling of pain or pressure in my head because I was convinced I was suddenly very stupid. Any time I made a simple mistake, or forgot to do something, I saw it as proof that it was really happening. I felt like a different person. I was taking my final two classes at the time, and schoolwork was impossible. I didn't trust my mind to be able to remember anything. I eventually dropped out of my classes. This was how powerful OCD was for me all of the sudden, and how much of an effect it had on my life.

I ended up talking to a professional at this point. It wasn't easy to try and explain that I felt like I was jinxed because of some shelves, but it was at this point I was told I have obsessive compulsive disorder. I was put on Paxil and started to attend an outpatient program for mental illness at the local hospital.

The Paxil definitely helped. Over time, I was a lot more relaxed. The feeling that I was suddenly a different person went away. My dad and I spent a few months in Colorado that summer, where Amy and Lori were now permanently living. I decided to finish my final two classes when I returned to Illinois in the fall. Lori's second child, Allison, was about to be born, nineteen months after her older sister, Kathryn. My dad and I drove out to meet her. On the fifteen-hour drive from Wheaton to Denver, I had issues reading a book that was at least partially responsible for my interest in writing—John Irving's *The World According to Garp*. Sometimes I got the compulsion to reread a word or section of the novel. At times, I would try to ignore it for a while, but it would bother me so much I would actually go back and reread the last five or so pages.

I remember a few things from this trip that both dealt with permanence. I bought a pair of sandals and had a bad feeling about them. I probably debated whether or not I wanted to return them. At one point, I set the clock on a microwave and felt as though I had to do it again. Because both of these things made me subconsciously worry about the future. The sandals I would own for years. As a matter of fact, I just threw them out a couple months ago, seven years later. I'm quite stylish. And the microwave clock would be set indefinitely.

I was just thinking this was the summer of 9/11, and I definitely have at least one OCD-related memory. On the day of the attacks, I said something to my sister along the lines of "Before all this World War III stuff started." A moment later, I had to follow it up with "Not World War III stuff" to make sure it was officially out there that 9/11 wasn't going to lead to World War III. I had anxiety as soon as I said "World War III," so I had to officially nip the war in the bud before it started (you're welcome).

By the time I came back to Wheaton in mid-September of '01, the Paxil had been in my system for several months, and I was feeling pretty good. Despite feeling far more relaxed in general, I still had some compulsions that were extreme at times. One compulsion from this time was to either get out of bed at night or completely leave my bedroom then come back into bed. I suppose I would worry about things as I was falling asleep and get anxious about the future. I somehow felt that getting out of and then back into my bed would superstitiously help with the things I was worried about. The reason I say this was a bit into the extreme is that my bedroom was now Lori and Amy's old room—the entire top floor of the house. So at times, I would actually get out of bed, walk all the way downstairs to the main floor, then go back into my room and get back into bed. There were some nights when I did this multiple times. For some reason, at times it was good enough if I just got out of bed, jumped off the ground for a second like an idiot, then laid back down. But when the worries were especially bad, I had to go all the way downstairs.

One final story from 2001 that goes along with the "You're just torturing yourself" strategy. In December, I began dating a girl named Heather. When she and I watched TV together, and I (as the hunter-gatherer) would be in charge of the remote, I would flip through the channels but feel the need to briefly go back to a previous channel. She never questioned me about it; she had no idea that I had OCD. (Years later I told her what was going on, and she said, "I thought you were trying to be funny.") It was early in the relationship, and I was concerned with making a good impression. I didn't want her to think I was some weirdo that changed channels for no reason or turned a lamp on and off several times (also something I did around her). So of course, my OCD found a little way to make myself appear strange(r than usual).

Chapter 6

The Real World and the Story
You've Been Waiting For

And since I haven't shared any funny stories in a while—during the fall of 2001, I had a job telemarketing magazine subscriptions while I took my final two classes. There were a few opening questions that we had to ask potential buyers. "How old are you? Are you married or single? Do you have any special interests or hobbies?" I decided to make it more interesting and add a final question, keeping a tally of people's responses. So I threw in "What's your favorite swear?" You may be surprised to know that "shit head" won. (Wait, maybe they were just calling me a shit head . . .)

As 2002 rolled around, my experience with compulsions stayed pretty much the same. I was still on Paxil and had things under control. There were small things I felt I had to repeat, but I'm not going to list them all. I spent some time traveling again, snowboarding with Chris and our friend Brad in Colorado, and then visiting the Gordons in California for the shooting of skeet and what have you. No ding-dong ditching this time around though. Here's a non-OCD related tip for you. When I started driving my dad's motorcycle on the highway, something I noticed when I stopped to pay tolls at unmanned booths on the interstate is that there's always a ton of change lying on the ground, where people missed the bucket. On the way to Colorado, we just opened the car door any time we had to pay tolls and picked up a handful of quarters off the ground. So don't bother paying tolls with your own money any more. Just open your door and take the change of those with poor aim. That's my one piece of advice that has nothing to do with

OCD or staying away from ecstasy. Well that, and if you're a dude, you should start flapping the schwing-schwong when you're seven or eight years old because that'll make it totally huge in adulthood.

I moved out of the house on Lyon Avenue at this time and into a nearby condo. The squirrels must have been disappointed. My mom really loved animals and made sure to throw a handful of peanuts in our backyard multiple times a day. This had some pretty funny consequences. For one thing, they became obese. Squirrels are usually so slim and fast, but years of living off an overabundance of peanuts made them all big and slow. Also, any time someone walked out of our back door, the squirrels came flocking for their peanuts in droves. It was like a scene out of *The Birds*. The bravest of squirrels would actually climb our back door and stare inside, waiting to be fed. At one point, our neighbor came over a few times a day to watch our pets while we were on vacation. She ended up calling her husband to help her leave because of the insane amount of squirrels acting as if they wanted to attack her when she approached the back door.

When May rolled around, it was time for me to finally start looking for a job. Unfortunately, it was also a time that I decided to try and quit taking Paxil. Something that can be seen often when people take antidepressants over a long stretch of time is they end up feeling great, so they think they don't need the drugs anymore. They feel relaxed and confident; they feel so good about themselves that it's like "Psh, I don't need any drugs. I feel fine now." The problem is you feel fine *because* of the drugs.

I had weaned myself off the medication while looking for a job in June. As the drugs wore off, the compulsions got worse. For example, I was also trying to write a short story at this time. If I got a bad feeling at the beginning of the day, about myself or the future, I wouldn't be able to spend any time writing that day. I felt as though I was jinxed, and any writing I did that day would be influenced by that magical bad feeling. I felt as though whatever bad thought I had about myself, it would be permanent if I added to my story on the same day. As if the story would then be infected, and any time I worked on it in the future would still be tainted by the cursed feeling.

At this point, I was $1,500 in debt and about to take a job selling vacuums as I kept going on interviews. I changed my mind because of another job offer before I was to start making presentations in people's homes, and I had to return the vacuum the company had given me. Of course, as I was leaving the building after returning the vacuum, I got a bad feeling about my intelligence and felt I had to reenter a room. I didn't; I just left and tried to ignore it. It was another case of feeling as though I was stupid all of the sudden, and I wanted to go back into the building to correct that and turn back into myself.

For several weeks, it was another "shelves in the closet" situation. I felt as if I was a new, far less intelligent person. I didn't want to reenter the building because that would have required me to make an excuse to awkwardly face these people whom I quit on after a day. Looking back now (and I'm sure, at the time, I had a sneaking suspicion), I know that's exactly why I picked walking into that building as a big important compulsion—to torture myself.

So I spent my time feeling like I was suddenly very stupid, similar to what had happened a year before with the shelves. Unfortunately, it was at a time that I started a new job. Chris hooked me up with a job fabricating Corian countertops with him. But as I learned my new responsibilities and stages in the production process, I felt as though I couldn't learn. I felt that leaving the magic vacuum building threw everything off, and I was going to lose my job because I didn't have the ability to learn or remember. It became true in a way—I was so convinced the magic could be real that I was in a constant state of worry and confusion.

It was a horrible feeling to again think that I suddenly had half a brain, so I found that my only escape was sleep. It was all I ever felt like doing—a way to escape reality and feel normal in my half-conscious states or dreams. There were some weekends that I wouldn't get out of bed until three or four in the afternoon. And even then, it was just because I had been in bed so long that I would feel extreme hunger when I dreamt.

Needless to say, I went back on the Paxil and felt like myself again. Eventually, I lost the desire to reenter the vacuum building.

But then my OCD started affecting my job performance. I felt I had to repeat various manufacturing tasks every day. I would turn sanders on and off multiple times, or maybe cut a piece of wood or Corian a certain length with a power saw, then get a bad feeling and have to recut it. Looking back on this now, it's interesting that those are the first two examples that come to mind. These actions made noise and drew attention to myself. So of course, I got a bad feeling and tortured myself into doing them again. I didn't want people to notice that I was repeating actions over and over, so what did I feel as though I had to repeat? Noisy actions.

We were on a tight schedule, and if I spent all day working on one project because I had to repeat things, I was at risk of losing my job. So my OCD slowed me down, but not to the point where I would get fired. Wow, what a coincidence! I'm lucky that the magical OCD fairies didn't bother me so much that I lost my job. But that's not true of course; it was all my choice, and all in my control. I had to repeat actions in such a way that it flirted with staying employed, but not quite enough to actually be reprimanded for it.

One day after work, I was talking to Chris online (this time as myself, not a fictitious girl I knocked up) about some recent changes on the job. A few temporary workers had been hired to help in the shop. One of them wasn't much help, and Chris said he wasn't going to be hired back. I typed "that's good, he pretty much just swept or stood around staring at people all day." Then I got the urge to keep sending that message. I sent it at least a couple additional times during that conversation, and I think I sent it again out of context the next day. He eventually asked, "Why do you keep saying that?" To which I responded, "It's a compulsive thing. Just ignore it." (None of my friends knew that I had OCD at this point, because I was wrongfully embarrassed about my strange thoughts.) I worried about my performance at work and about what kind of contribution I was making. So when I typed a sentence about someone not returning to work because he wasn't working hard enough, it gave me a bad feeling. Subconsciously it made me worry about keeping my job, so I distracted myself from that thought by retyping a sentence.

I had a lot of issues with buying things at this time. Seems like every time I went to the grocery store to pick up a few things, I would deal with bad feelings about the specific products I chose. I'd grab a bag of grapes, have a superstitious feeling about the future or myself, and put it back to choose another. I think there was actually something I eventually exchanged, several days later. Not food from the grocery store, but maybe a little camera I got for Kathryn's third birthday. I had it at home for a few days, convinced it would make the future bad, until I finally took it back to the store and exchanged it for a safer, less magical one. Of course, this toy would be something she had for several years, so the bad feeling was a lot harder to deal with than a feeling I may have gotten about a bag of grapes that I'd finish in a week.

It was around this time that I began my "loophole" strategy. At this point, I had been on Paxil for several months, so I was feeling quite good in general. Similar to the way I felt after several months on Paxil in 2001, towards the end of my long Colorado trip. If I got the urge to repeat an action, I would say in my mind "If I do that again, the devil may have my soul." So of course, that scared me into not repeating the action. Even if I got a really bad feeling and actually felt as though I needed to repeat some meaningless action, I could just say in my mind, for example, "God, or anyone listening, if I cut that piece of Corian again, Satan may have my soul when I die."

Perhaps this could work as a strategy for you. If you're religious, you could make a pact with God that if you repeat a certain action for no reason, it means you want something terrible to happen. Say, for example, you want to return to a room to magically ensure you don't get AIDS. Instead, say in your mind to any magical forces at work, "If I go back into that room, that will mean that I want to get/want God to give me AIDS."

Eventually, however, there were problems with this strategy. Sometimes, if I got a bad feeling about something before I did it, I would try this soul chant strategy. I recall a time when I was driving home after doing some errands, and there were a few different routes for me to go. I picked the way I wanted to go, then got a bad feeling about it, as though the future would be affected negatively if I went home that way. Since I was so used to this new strange strategy, I quickly thought, "If I don't go home that way, Satan may have my soul." And then there was some road construction, and that route wasn't an option. So I announced in my mind, "Well, regardless of what I said before, I didn't mean it. Now Satan can have my soul unless I go home this other way." After things like that started happening, the whole strategy became a grey area. Eventually, if I got a real bad feeling about, let's say, an article of clothing I put on, and I couldn't handle it, I would eventually cancel out what I had said in my mind. "No matter what I said before, now I'm saying that if I don't change to a different pair of boxers, Satan can have my soul. And this time I mean it. I didn't mean what I said before."

Keep in mind that I didn't even really believe I was praying to any kind of forces. This may be evident by my lazy attitude regarding breaking the promises I was declaring in my mind. It's just the form my OCD takes. My strategies to avoid repeating myself and reasons for repeating actions in the first place all had a theme of fearing a God or hell I wasn't sure I even believed in at this point in my life.

2003 was, until Autumn, a fairly good year for me and my experience with OCD. Paxil had been in my system for a full year. I felt happy, relaxed, and confident. My "soul" strategy worked, for the most part. I even had some kind of religious awakening in the spring. I was happy, and I felt confident that there was a God taking care of me. This was reflected in the short stories I was writing at the time. They had themes of God, love, and the beauty of life.

During the summer, I moved into a house in Chicago with two friends. I was suddenly paying my own rent and working a job as an estimator for a granite company. It didn't pay exceptionally well (I just got the urge to take this sentence out for superstitious reasons, because it stirred up anxiety about money). Also, the psychiatrist I was seeing was back in Wheaton, almost an hour west of Chicago. So I decided, yet again, to stop taking medication. It led to what was by far my worst experience with OCD.

At first, I just became depressed. The Paxil was gone, so my imbalance was back, and I felt very depressed most of the time. Some weekends, I would go to bed at 9:00 p.m. and not get out of bed until one the next afternoon, just out of boredom and a general feeling of "blah". I didn't get pleasure out of anything I did.

Part of depression for me, which seriously messed with my religiously themed OCD, are feelings of anger and darkness. When I'm depressed and dislike life, I start "turning towards the dark side," so to speak. I don't feel happy; I don't feel like believing in some kind of loving God. I get turned on by thoughts of evil or demonic possession. Analyzing this from a scientific point of view, it's just anger at life. Not that there really is a God or Satan, but feeling "bad" is an attractive option since childhood. It's rebellious to be naughty or to go against what your parents tell you. But at this point in my life, I thought there was a chance that God, Satan, the afterlife, and demonic possession were all real.

So my OCD moved from the outside world into my thoughts. Instead of repeating actions, I was more concerned with my thoughts. Not so much repeating them (that will be a problem come 2006), but more so that they were influenced by Satan. For example, if I was trying to remember something but was having trouble—let's say a name from the past—for a split second I would think that I was using, or that I wanted to use Satan's help to come up with the name. I'd get this weird, dark, confident feeling, and the name would suddenly come to mind.

Spooky as that may sound, I was just messing with myself. Tricking myself into thinking Satan was putting thoughts into my mind so that I would get all worked up about it for a while. It's just confidence. The power of the mind. As I touched upon earlier, if you believe you can do something, you can. So I believed I would be able to come up with the name, and I would. No one put the name in my mind. On some level, I already knew that. I think at times I caught myself thinking about how much better off I would have been if man had never invented the idea of God and Satan. But of course, I had to worry and apologize to God, and maybe repeat the action by remembering a different name from the past, this time feeling as though I was using only God's help.

Another example is playing video games with my friends. If I felt like I was using Satan's help, then performed well, I would have to make sure and play it again, this time concentrating on using just God's help. Similarly, if I tried to work on a story, I would worry about evil forces helping me. If I made myself feel like Satan was helping me, I would suddenly come up with a well thought-out sentence, or a good way to phrase something. So my writing completely stopped at this time.

This may not sound very much like OCD to you at this point. Hopefully, you didn't pick up a self-help book because you couldn't stop washing your hands, only to read a story about a guy who's afraid of Lucifer putting thoughts into his brain. It's true, when I checked myself into a mental health facility in late '03, the doctor I talked to said there was more going on than just OCD, and I was put on the antipsychotic Risperdal because of my obsession with and fear of demonic forces. (Although, it was the same doctor that thought I didn't have OCD because I would walk around in my socks, and to her that meant I wasn't afraid of germs and therefore didn't have OCD. Most of the people from the survey I conducted knew more about OCD than she did. But it was a state-run facility, so it's not like I was going to be talking to Jason Seaver.) But these are still OCD traits, and hopefully, it can relate to your experience.

So my compulsions got out of hand because I wanted to feel like someone that didn't have an attraction to dark feelings. The problem was, no little action was going to kill away that part of me, because it's just who I am. I remember performing an action at work on a Friday afternoon, then feeling like I was someone that wanted to be possessed by a demon. So I tried to repeat the action, but the feeling wouldn't go away. Part of me must have thought it might be cool to be taken over by an evil force. So I drove home and tried to come to terms with the fact that I'm somebody that might want to be possessed and tried to convince myself that didn't necessarily mean that I was going to be possessed or that I was going to hell when I died.

At work, all my tasks started taking probably four times as long as they should. My work would pile up, and that would just increase my stress level many times over. My job suddenly had new responsibilities, and I was running out of money. I needed a raise soon; otherwise, I was just going to slowly go into debt. So now I had to worry that I would actually lose my job, and that made my anxiety and OCD even worse. I would have to look at certain pages of blueprints multiple times. I would have to discreetly enter and leave the bathroom over and over until I got a good feeling about things. I found myself fighting the urge to repeat myself on the phone.

I tried getting back on medication, but it was almost as if it were too late. My initial reaction to drugs was even more anxiety. I suppose if I had kept taking them, I would have gotten past the initial side effect of increased anxiety, but I didn't have the patience for that. OCD was already disrupting my life too much, and the medication just took it to a new level.

Thanksgiving of 2003 was when the compulsions were more extreme than ever before. I dropped one of my roommates off at Midway Airport to fly to his girlfriend's hometown in Minnesota. On the way back, I got a bad feeling when I last stepped in a gas station parking lot, but tried to ignore it and made my way to Wheaton. A few days later, it had bothered me constantly, and I decided to drive all the way back to the gas station near Midway (forty-five minutes maybe). The entire drive, I kept getting bad feelings and driving over the same area on the highway. I would take an exit just to retrace my route, and several times, I felt it wasn't good enough, so I had to keep going back.

I returned to Chicago and went to work for one more week before I decided to seek help. Things were pretty out of hand. I would drive home and end up circling our block several times until it felt right. I stopped doing laundry, even though almost all of my clothes needed to be washed, because I knew I would be repeating every little action and, quite possibly, doing the same load of laundry multiple times. Sleeping was almost impossible. I kept a Bible under my pillow, and every once in a while, I would have to get out of bed and walk out of our back door for a second.

I finally decided to check my self into a mental health facility. I don't know if this was an extreme move or not. I probably should have just stuck with the medication and worked through the extra anxiety it caused me at first. I don't know why I thought a mental institution would be some kind of cure-all for my problems. I pictured a few weeks of intense therapy and medication, and then emerging as a different person with OCD under control. My experience there wasn't like that at all. I talked to a doctor maybe once a week for half an hour; the rest of the time, I just sat around, watching television or reading a book. They put me on a heavy regiment of Zoloft, Ativan, and Risperdal. This slowly helped, but of course, it takes time.

The morning I decided to check in was a long and tedious one. It took me forever to leave the house; I kept having to walk over the same area on one of our rugs. I finally got to work half an hour late and talked to my boss about OCD being out of control. I kept driving over the same area on the way home. I think I was extra stressed this day because I felt as though I was about to check in to an institute that would cure me, but if I had a bad or Satanic feeling on the way there, my entire experience with recovery would be tainted with that.

So I spent two weeks in the facility, repeating actions and adjusting to medication. Analyzing the actions I was repeating while I was there from this point in my life five years later, it's obvious I was just trying to make things more difficult for myself. I was worried about what my fellow patients would think of me, so I made a fool out of myself repeating actions involving them. Some girl gave me a Coke at one point, and I said thanks, then got a bad feeling and had to say thanks a few more times. So I sounded like an idiot, repeating myself because my severe OCD wasn't something I was explaining to everyone. In the middle of the night, I would get a bad feeling and have to briefly leave my room. There were people working at the front desk who could observe me doing this. So of course, I was drawing attention to myself. Who knows, if I could have walked in and out of my room without being seen, my compulsion might have been limited to getting in and out of bed.

At one point, I was suddenly given a new roommate. When he was getting settled in our room, I said something to him and got a bad feeling. It bothered me to the point where several minutes later, I actually asked him to come back into our room for a second so I could repeat what I had said. So of course, my roommate thought I was quite odd. Although, I did explain to him that I had severe OCD, and he didn't seem to think it was so outrageous. Also, I felt the need to repeat eye contact with random people in the main room at times. Of course I did—that way, I could look foolish making an effort to look into people's eyes repeatedly.

One compulsion I performed at this time goes back to the "it's never anything too inappropriate" strategy. I often would get the urge to repeat myself on the phone. They had a pay phone in the main room, so I was talking to my dad, sisters, coworkers, or friends about my situation from time to time. At one point, after I talked to Lori, I had the urge to repeat something I said during our conversation, and it was so strong that I called her back after maybe half an hour. Did OCD ever make me call my boss or dad back? No, I would have found that too embarrassing. So I only had to sound like a fool to someone that knew a lot about OCD—someone I was closer to and who I wouldn't be embarrassed about exposing a compulsion to.

And even as OCD was disrupting my life this much, to the point where I risked losing my job and spent two weeks in this facility, deep down, I felt that the entire disorder was nothing more than me messing with myself. But I couldn't help it; it's the way my brain is wired, and it all felt very real. At one point, I was in an MRI machine, being scanned to see if my mental issues were caused by anything physical. I just lay there wondering how much it cost for them to scan me all because I was doing something that's the equivalent of stabbing myself in the leg all day long just to torture myself. But we can't help it, can we? You wash your hands for that hundredth time and know it's illogical and pointless, but knowing that is not going to stop you.

After two weeks I was released, spent the holidays in Colorado, and came back to work in January. I still had problems, and while it wasn't nearly as bad as before I had checked in, it still bothered me all day. On a typical day, my alarm would go off, and I would immediately worry that Satan was going to tell me what time exactly to get out of bed. I'd be lying there, and if 6:04 flashed in my mind, I'd have to try and make sure to get out of bed at 6:05 instead. I would drive to work and get bad feelings every time I changed lanes. When scanning the radio for songs, I would sometimes torture myself into feeling like I wanted to use Satan's help to find a good song before I changed stations. So if I felt that way, then changed stations and it was a song I liked, I had to change the station and not listen to the song that DJ Satan picked just for me. And of course, I don't control such big things. My thoughts don't influence what songs get played on the radio. Obviously, there wasn't a certain song playing that suddenly changed because of my strange thoughts. And in reality, any good feeling I had about an upcoming song was either a coincidence or my subconscious mind being aware of patterns regarding the songs that are played on certain stations at certain times.

Here are a few last examples along these lines. When deciding what I wanted to have for dinner when I got home from work, it was just like getting out of bed. I worried that Satan was putting ideas for meals in my mind. At night, maybe I would try and watch a movie. But if I felt like I wanted to use Satan's help to enjoy it, I had to stop watching.

You get the idea. Or it all just sounds like illogical, ridiculously stupid insanity to you. Either way, time to talk about 2004. The company I was working for wasn't doing very well financially. There were days that I didn't have to come in at all, and sometimes, I would come in for just half a day. Then we lost one of our major accounts, and I was laid off. I decided to move in with Lori's family (which had been expanded to include a son, Blake) in Kremmling, Colorado.

CHAPTER 7

And the Rest

So I headed out to Colorado and started working at a ski resort. OCD seemed to slowly fade away. After a few months, I stopped taking the medication I was on, and even then, I was pretty much all right. I still had little urges to repeat things, but I think the "Satan may have my soul if I do that again" strategy worked, because I just wasn't very anxious about things. Must have been the high altitude. That and the fact that I was pretty depressed. This time around, depression actually helped with anxiety and OCD. When you're depressed, you don't care about much of anything, so you're not going to do a lot of worrying. I don't know why that wasn't my reaction to depression a year earlier, that would have been nice. It probably had something to do with the fact that in Kremmling, I didn't have to worry about losing my job or paying rent. Little things still bothered me. For example, if I took the kids to the park, I might get a bad feeling about using an evil force to help me push one of them on the swings. Then if that ended up being the last push of the day, it would make me worry for a while. But I would get over it. It wasn't anything I was about to check myself in to a mental institution over.

One story worth mentioning involves Blake. He was about a year old at this time, and he had to have surgery because one of his testicles had not yet descended. Several years before this, my mom kept a small stuffed animal in her car—a porcupine. I don't remember where it came from, but for years it was tucked into part of the dashboard as her copilot.

The night before the surgery, Lori had a dream in which she was talking to my mom. It ended with my mom saying "I have to go watch over Blake" and leaving the room. After the surgery was successful, a nurse came out and gave Blake a little gift—another stuffed porcupine, same exact model as my mom's dashboard travel companion.

Pretty comforting story, I would say. Similarly, not long after my mom died, Lori had a dream where they were having a conversation. It ended with my mom saying, "I'm outside all the time now," and this woke Lori up because it didn't seem as though it was part of the dream; it sounded more like it was actually spoken by someone in her bedroom. Anyone that knew my mom well would tell you that her ideal heaven would be spending time outdoors. She spent the vast majority of her weekends doing yard work, planting flowers or vegetables and making sure the front and backyard looked perfect. She grew up in California, hated cold weather, and was extremely happy every year when spring came around.

You might say if I find these stories comforting because I think it's possible that my mom was communicating with Lori, that means I'm a hypocrite. Writing about how there is no God, heaven, or hell, and then implying Annette was talking to Lori from her ideal heaven. But as I'll discuss soon when I address my father's death, I have a different view of a possible afterlife. I think it's possible the dead can communicate from a different dimension, or they're energy or conscious always exists somewhere. Possibly. And at the same time, if she was communicating from an ideal afterlife or watching over Blake, that just proves that the Christian Bible is kaput. Because according to what it says, anyone who denounces God goes to hell, no matter what. (Then again, it also says anyone who curses their parents or works on a Sunday must be "put to death.")

Most of the stories I have involving Blake are pretty humorous. Kids are constantly supply of funny stories. Just a few months ago, I was home alone with Blake, and he called me into the bathroom to wipe his bum. I was under the impression that he had been doing that himself for a while, but apparently, he was just quiet about asking his parents for help when other people were around.

"Can't you just do it yourself?" I asked.

"I don't want to."

"Why not?"

"It's boring."

On a different occasion, Blake and Allison were watching TV by themselves and saw a commercial for Moon Sand, a kind of sculpting clay. Blake paused it when the number to call came onscreen because he wanted some Moon Sand delivered to his house. Soon enough, Lori heard Blake crying, so she came into the room to see what was going on. She assumed they were probably fighting.

"What happened?" she asked Allison.

"The Moon Sand people told him he doesn't have any money."

After about a year and a half, I had enough of Kremmling and moved back to a condo in Buffalo Grove, Illinois, to hang out with my friends again. I'll keep rushing forward through time pretty quickly here because OCD wasn't much of a problem. I think a lot of that had to do with the fact that several years had passed since my mom died. I was starting to come to terms with that and had much less anxiety over the concept of a parent dying. Little things still bothered me, similar to pushing kids on the swings a year before. For example, if I was playing baseball with a few friends in a field near our condo, I would make sure and try to feel like I was using only God's help sometimes before I pitched or swung. If I felt like I used Satan's help, especially before a good hit, I felt the need to repeat it. But much like pushing kids on the swings, I would get over it pretty quickly if I wasn't given a chance to repeat myself.

In December of '05, my dad informed me he had been diagnosed with myelodysplastic syndrome—a blood cell disorder that's a death sentence unless you have a successful bone marrow transplant. So in case you thought my OCD was fading away since we had moved so far away from my mother's death, don't worry, it's coming back with a vengeance in about a year.

In February of 2006, I wrote a short story, and I could tell that my OCD was more or less in remission. When deciding how to phrase sentences, I would worry that evil forces were putting thoughts into my mind or helping. But it was very easy to ignore. I felt confident that I was just messing with myself, and no outside influence was actually helping me write. Even if I got a bad feeling, or a dark and confident urge came over me and I was suddenly able to create a well constructed sentence, I would briefly announce in my mind that if I went back and changed it, Satan could have my soul. And that was easily a good enough strategy at this point. I was fairly confident that it was all fake.

In the spring of 2006, something happened that demonstrated how little I cared about OCD, or how little I believed that my strange thoughts were valid. For years, I had been using the "devil may have my soul if I repeat that" strategy. Then one day at work, I felt the urge to repeat some action, thought of the soul strategy in my mind, and repeated the action anyway. Not because it bothered me so much that I had to repeat it, but more along the lines of "Oh yeah? Big deal. Watch this . . . . ooooh, I guess Satan can have your soul now! Idiot." But then, of course, I did feel a little anxious afterwards.

This lead to the "time is on your side" strategy that I very much recommend for you. For maybe a month, the "soul" strategy obviously didn't work because it fell apart. I messed with it. But then I decided to officially stop repeating actions. I had one final bad feeling (choosing a box of envelopes at the store, I wanted to put it back and pick another), and I ignored it. It wasn't too difficult for me to do because OCD was practically in remission. But it really works wonders if you're able to stick to it. Every time I got a bad feeling, I would think to myself that I was trying to quit and trying to go as long as I could without repeating actions.

To repeat what I said in the intro, the reason this works so well is that with time, it just becomes more and more powerful. At first, it's "Come on, you've gone a few weeks without repeating anything, don't give that up now." Then eventually, it's months, or even a year. You build up many experiences ignoring really powerful urges to perform compulsions. If you make it months without repeating anything, you don't want to give that all up. You don't want all that work to be for nothing. And when you get really bad feelings, you think, "I've ignored plenty of really bad feelings over the past six months, I'm not going to give in to this one. After a few days, I'll go back to feeling like myself."

That's also part of the strategy that proves how fake everything is. Even now as I write this, in the recent past I've been dealing with some pretty powerful negative feelings and urges to repeat actions. I wrote down a number while balancing my checkbook a few months ago and got a bad feeling about being evil or about being attracted to sick thoughts. It was at a time when I was watching a program about serial killers. (Technically, it was about the psychology of Batman, but they were talking about serial killers at the time.) They were showing headlines on the screen about such killers as Ted Bundy and Jeffrey Dahmer. So I focused on the sick, tiny part of me that I keep tucked away in my subconscious that might think the idea of psychos is kind of attractive and multiplied any feeling of excitement I may have had a thousand fold just to torture myself. I think everyone has dark thoughts lurking in his or her brain, but we choose right from wrong. We know what's good overall, regardless of what might be lurking in small regions of our brains. I have no real desire to be evil, but some tiny part of me must be at least curious. (That's not just me, right?)

So I felt as though I had to write a certain number again, but I chose to ignore it. So of course, everything felt "off" for a few days. But eventually, with time, I just forgot about it. Several new urges took its place. A few days after the Batman evil number incident, I got a strange feeling after cracking my knuckle on my steering wheel while I was driving. Of course, as I was fighting the urge to repeat it, I didn't even think about the checkbook-balancing-serial-killer fiasco. It just magically went away, as though there was no doubt in my mind that it was fake the whole time.

This strategy that started in maybe April of '06, after the envelopes, when I built up time and didn't let myself repeat actions, lasted for about exactly a year. However, in the meantime, OCD found a new way to mess with me. I never officially made a rule about repeating thoughts. And it wouldn't have mattered if I did, because it's damn near impossible to not repeat a thought. So while I was busy making sure to never repeat any actions, I came to another stressful period in my life, and I had to repeat thoughts instead. (And I must warn you, this is where I'm extra concerned about giving you new ideas for your OCD. Because torturing yourself into repeating thoughts/ memories/math/emotions sucks a fat one.)

It was mid-August of 2006 when I officially found out my dad wasn't going to make it. They tried a bone marrow transplant in early July. Not something they would usually attempt for anyone older than thirty, but he was in very good shape for a sixty-one-year-old aside from the disease (or he had a good insurance plan and a lot of money).

This time around, I had a more mature and realistic view of death, compared to when I was a kid afraid his mommy was going to a mythical fiery place. I thought it was possible he was going to experience some kind of afterlife. Not so much sitting on clouds above us with all of the good people who have died, but maybe an existence in a different dimension where he, in a sense, could watch over us and, perhaps, even communicate with the living—subconsciously or in dreams. Maybe reincarnation, maybe his energy would continue in some form. Or maybe he would just stop existing. Long story short, I wasn't repeating anything to make sure he went to the Christian heaven when he died.

I came out to Colorado just before he died and left after his funeral. At this point, Blake was three, so he had several questions about death and what happens to people after they die. We did our best to try and make him understand. After the service, everyone drove to the cemetery for his military burial. Blake got out of the limo, looked around at all the grass and headstones, and disappointedly asked, "*This* is heaven?"

I returned back to work in Illinois for maybe a month, but soon moved to Colorado for a second time. Now living without a roommate, I found myself alone with my thoughts, day in and day out. That, combined with the stress of another parent dying, gave OCD a whole new format. I remember a time in late 2006 when I first saw one of my all-time favorite movies, *Donnie Darko*. The next day, I was remembering the well-known actors in the movie and ended on Noah Wyle and got a bad feeling. So I had to keep repeating "Noah Wyle" in my mind until I got a good feeling, the same way I used to repeat actions. The difficult part about this was how hard it is to not think of something. So even when I thought the name and got a good feeling about the future, I would think it again, just to torture myself.

That's how the thought repeating started. Over time, it got more complex. Shortly after the *ER* doc incident, I had to think of as many rhymes as I could for a certain word. I don't remember what word it was, but it was the same situation. If I thought of a bunch and got a bad feeling, I would have to try and come up with one I had yet to think of and hope to get a good feeling about the future at that time. This lead to me torturing myself almost any time I tried to remember anything. Let's say for example I was trying to remember as many fellow students as I could from some class I had in middle school. Same situation—if I got a bad feeling after I landed on a name, I would have to remember someone else in the class.

Math was another issue. Any time I had to perform simple math, like when I was balancing my checkbook or thinking of how many years ago something happened, I had to repeat it over and over. And of course, the "Satan's help" worry affected this new form of OCD as well. Not only did I have to repeat things in my mind until I got a good feeling, sometimes I would have to repeat them because I felt like Satan was helping me do math in my mind or helping me to remember an example of something.

By the way, I know it makes no sense to write a book that's borderline blasphemous and then admit to having all these fears of Satan and hell. As I tried to explain in the intro, I don't really believe these things; there are just lingering shades of belief that frighten me. Plus, it's just the form that my OCD takes on. If man had never invented the idea of Satan, OCD would affect me as much and be just as stressful; it would just be more about the future and maybe other paranormal fears. You may also feel that worrying about Satan influencing my thoughts is something separate from OCD. But I'm still repeating actions and repeating thoughts to make the future better, which is what OCD is all about. You can get an unspecific superstitious bad feeling, or you can feel as though you need to repeat an action because it was influenced by a demon. Either way, you're repeating an action to undo a curse, which makes no logical sense. If a demon helped a person do something, why would repeating that action without the demon's help make everything better and cancel out the demon's help or curse? Only a person with OCD would think that way.

So this thought-repeating situation got pretty out of hand. For a few months, I felt as though all I did was wake up in the morning, deal with severe OCD in my mind all day, then go back to bed, and do it all over again the next day. Sometimes it got so bad and I felt so stressed out that I literally just forced myself to completely stop for a few hours, because I just couldn't handle the anxiety and constant repeating of thoughts, and I really began to fear for my mental health and stress level. Which I guess is a strategy in itself. Obviously I know it's fake if I can take a break from it because I'm concerned for my well-being.

Over time, the mental rituals got easier. They were exceptionally bad the first six months or so after my dad died. Since then, they've died down a lot. It's another example of what happened after my mom died—years passed, and OCD died down. I still feel the need to repeat thoughts, but it's nowhere the extreme it was in late 2006/early 2007. (I think part of that is due to the fact that my brain is fried from all the anxiety and depression, so I'm really not able to think of much anything at all.)

As I said earlier, the "no repeating actions" rule I started in April of 2006 only lasted a year. In April of 2007, for some reason, I slowly started repeating actions again. It was a gradual slope that probably started right after my dad died, around the same time the thoughts started acting up. At first, it was okay to repeat actions such as looking at things or blinking because it's very hard to stop yourself from doing such simple little actions. It's almost like trying not to think a certain thought. Soon enough, anything limited to my body was okay to repeat, like certain movements or the cracking of a joint. There were certain other actions that became okay to repeat, but it would be hard to explain it all. Eventually, I felt as though I had let so many "repeats" slide that I was just fooling myself, and I started having serious issues repeating little everyday actions until a few months later in July when I felt I couldn't take it anymore.

At that point, I decided I needed to try to completely stop actions again. I reread a book about OCD and decided to officially stop the actions once again. There was a little chart included in my OCD workbook where every day, I would write down the compulsions I wanted to act out. This is strategy number 2, and it seems to work quite well. Reading the OCD book itself helps because it puts you in a different frame of mind. You are constantly reminded that your OCD is a specific mental disorder, and that the magical rules are not real. And when you're officially trying to stick to a plan, with a chart to mark your progress, it's the whole "building up days" strategy.

That basically brings us up to date. I've never been big on conclusions. I think I've said everything I wanted to say. If you weren't paying attention, you're a butt. Writing this book has been very therapeutic for me. I've spent eight months writing it and analyzing my own OCD. As a result, I see it much more as a disorder than as strange forces that may be real. The magic now feels much less real. I hope that this book had the same effect on you. As I mentioned, that's the ultimate strategy. Please try and apply my analysis and strategies to your experience with OCD so that these past seven and a half years of stress from this ridiculous disorder can be for something.

I'm not sure that there's any way to completely kill away OCD. It's the way our brains are wired; it's the chemical imbalances in our heads. Of course, that's incredibly frustrating. It affected me while writing this book many, many times. (Ironically enough, I spent all day today reading this one final time before sending it to my publisher, and OCD was in high gear the entire time. Of course, because I'm about to submit a book about how crazy and stupid I am, and I want to make it sound exactly the way I want it.) What we can do is try and understand it. Try and understand why we're messing with ourselves, why we have so much guilt, etc. Just know that superstitions are all fake. Any time it seems like a superstition works, it's coincidence.

You have to remember that the universe does not revolve around you. You don't direct accidents and disease. You don't prevent tragedy. All things considered, you really don't control much of anything. And that's kind of scary—that leads to OCD in the first place. But stop it with your rituals and superstitions already. It's all just very childish.

And at this point in my life, here's the strategy that I find works best—body movements are okay to repeat, but no actions unless you repeat it immediately—if more than a few seconds have passed, no repeating it. But it's okay to repeat an action as long as you wait until a specified day of the week (it's Thursday mornings for me). That may have made sense or will work for one or two people out there that just happen to have almost the same exact form of OCD as I do.

Good luck to you.

www.ingramcontent.com/pod-product-compliance
Lightning Source LLC
Chambersburg PA
CBHW031304280526
45784CB00004B/1982